Copyright © 2005-2006 Olivia Qusaibaty.

Typeset in Times New Roman
Printed and bound in the United States of America

First printed 2006

ISBN 1-4196-4446-7

I0449471

Media Under Pressure: Al-Jazeera Toeing the Red Lines

To Ammar

Olivia Qusaibaty

Table of Contents

Olivia Qusaibaty

Introduction

In the transnational context, as defined by intensified flows of individuals, commercial goods and services, institutions, and ideas, the seemingly diametrically opposed subject and object of discourse encounter each other more often and with growing intensity. The result, which some have called "the end of history" (Fukuyama 1992) and others "the clash of civilizations" (Huntington 1993, 1996), represents competing trends between processes of assimilation and differentiation, while cultural globalisation literature tends to describe certain cultural forms and styles as the "hybrid" products of multidirectional cultural flows ascribed to "no particular locality." (Tomlinson 1998: 138). As global integration emerges on the forefront of contemporary discussion, denoting a two-way flow, power relations between different global actors retain their immediacy. The media sector offers a compelling illustration of this phenomenon.

The rise to international notoriety of Qatar-based Arabic-language satellite news channel *Al-Jazeera,* fostered by the plurality of responses it has received, provides an example of the continued saliency of polarized discourse in the media and other sectors. Throughout this study of the satellite channel, particular attention has been given to patterns of and pressures for change in the Arab world. The broadcaster's reach, however, extends into the living rooms of Arabic and non-Arabic speakers alike spread across the globe. (Allied Media 2005) Although at times using the Arab world as a frame of reference, this work does not consider it a unified entity as such. Important political, social, economic, cultural and religious differences mark the region. Notably, censorship, though widespread in the Arab world, differs depending on the government or regime. Censorship in Morocco, Egypt, and Jordan is more lenient than under more authoritarian regimes in countries such as Algeria, Tunisia, Libya, Iraq, and Syria. (Hafez 2001) A single message or program produces a wide spectrum of responses. The analysis curtails its approach accordingly.

The sudden significance of CNN in the first Gulf War, its evident pro-Western news spin and the lack of alternatives provided an impetus for media development in the Arab world. (Gaballah 2005; Miles 2005; El-Nawawy and Iskandar 2002; Sakr 2001) A distinctive Arab voice broadcast out of an Arab country and reflecting Arab opinions while also borrowing some of the look and feel of Western news television, (El-Nawawy and Iskandar 2002) Al-Jazeera has the potential to facilitate reciprocity. In tackling sensitive issues in its reports and talk shows, the channel has provided a platform for debate in the Arab world and beyond. This work evaluates Al-Jazeera's ability to provide a perspective other than that of its Western and Arab competitors on current and past world events and to provide a public space of dialogue free of control and censorship. Both of these elements constitute the main features of Al Jazeera's media model and motto, *al-ra'y wal-ra'y al-akhar* (the opinion and the other opinion.)[1] In contrast, much of the literature on Al-Jazeera has adopted a generalized approach and has been tinted with a strong positive or negative bias toward the news channel.

---

[1] Translation by the author here and for all subsequent French and Arabic quotes or titles. Arabic words and names are transcribed phonetically so as to best represent their classical Arabic pronunciation.

Olivia Qusaibaty

Chapter 1 establishes the channel's position within the current global media scene while chapter 2 examines the channel's contribution to creating a public space for dialog, especially as relates to the Arab world. Original qualitative data supporting the study features a framing analysis applied to three selected programs over a set period of time (January and March 2005) in chapter 3. Chapters 4 and 5 provide several examples of the sharp criticism Al-Jazeera has received in its attempts to abide by its dichotomous model (voicing the opinion and its opposite). Previous to concluding remarks to this research, chapter 6 establishes whether the channel has indeed provided the opinion and the other opinion. Additional empirical research includes interviews with a number of regular viewers as well as correspondents and members of the channel's editorial team. The author has followed the broadcaster's coverage since 2001 and has watched the channel for an average of 6 hours per day at different timeslots between December 2004 and August 2005.

1. What is Al-Jazeera Today?

Since its launch in November 1996, Arabic language satellite television news channel Al-Jazeera has managed to fundamentally challenge and alter the Arab world's mediascape by giving voice to government criticism previously suppressed in the region's mass media. (El-Nawawy and Iskandar 2002) The channel's exclusive news coverage, heated political debates, and in-depth documentaries at first startled audiences used to censorship and the regular feed of Egyptian soap operas, old films, government-sponsored news and other entertainment emanating from official or government-affiliated outlets. The largest and most controversial channel in the Middle East, Al-Jazeera offers news coverage 24 hours a day focusing on the hottest regions of conflict as well as a number of political documentaries, talk shows, and debates. Seven talk shows broadcast live from various locations on a weekly basis in primetime. In addition to non-primetime shows, numerous other programs are presented as specials, broadcast with relevance to current events. Recorded history, culture and health shows also appear regularly, in addition to live business and sports bulletins (see Table 4. Main Live and Recorded Al-Jazeera Programs). A daily review of the world press, an economics and business report from London, the New York Stock Exchange and sometimes other exchange markets, are featured. The channel's network also comprises three sports channel (the direct-to-home Al Jazeera Sports Plus-1 and Al-Jazeera Sports Plus-2 were launched on *Al-Jazeera Mubashir*—a channel providing 24-hour live coverage of events—, and a documentary channel. A children's channel is planned to begin broadcast in late 2005 while the projected launch in March 2006 of the English-language *Al-Jazeera International* (AJI), will determine the organization's place in the English-language international news environment. (Psenny 2005; Wallis 2005) The first English-language news channel based in the Middle East, AJI plans to compete with CNN International and BBC World, the world's leading global English-language broadcasters. All Al-Jazeera channels except for the direct-to-home subscription only channels Al-Jazeera Sports Plus-1 and Al-Jazeera Sports Plus-2 (launched August 27, 2005) are available free-to-air in Arab countries.

25 members of the channel's initial core editorial team worked for the BBC Arabic channel before the latter's run-in with the Saudi Arabian government. A total of 120 journalists, broadcasters, and technicians of the 250 rendered jobless by the terminated BBC Arabic/Orbit contract joined Al-Jazeera. (Miles 2005) Their Western training and presentation style has profoundly impacted the nature of Al-Jazeera broadcasts, fuelled by 24 bureaus and numerous internationally located correspondents. Aired every hour on the hour, news broadcasts rely on the channel's numerous correspondents around the world, but also on predominantly Western news agencies. Al-Jazeera subscribes to Reuters and APTN for its images, and the AP, AFP, Deutsche Presse Agentur (DPA), Middle East News Agency (MENA), Reuters and Qatar News Agency (QNA) newswires. The Emir of Qatar, Hamad bin Khalifa Al Thani, who assumed his position as Qatari head of state in a peaceful *coup d'état* against his father, Sheikh Khalifa bin Hamad Al Thani, in June 1995, disbursed an initial loan of five hundred million Qatari riyals (approximately $137 million) to cover Al-Jazeera's first five years of operation. The channel was then expected to reach financial independence through advertising, the sale of programs and footage as well as through the loan of equipment to other television stations. Although it functions independently from the Qatari government, Al-Jazeera, which broadcasts continuously since January 1, 1999, continues to depend on government funding for financial support, a situation that has drawn criticism and allegations that the channel follows self-censorship when reporting issues sensitive to Qatar. (Bahry 2001; Al-Ghamdy 2005)

Despite its seeming breaching of taboos, the channel does operate within certain red lines. Al-Jazeera Deputy Chief Editor Ayman Gaballah explains that "there is nothing with no ceiling, but this [Al-Jazeera] is the highest ceiling, and I think that even compared to the Western news, this is the highest ceiling." (Gaballah 2005) Yet, as Sakr argues, "with the emirate's political reform program having been devised by the emir himself, and with Al-Jazeera seen as an element in that program, an alignment between the state and the satellite channel was perceived both internally and externally." (Sakr 2001: 59) Reflecting the channel's editorial response to this critique, Washington bureau chief reporter Mohammed al-Alami argued that "the Qatari government is under tremendous pressure from [the American] government here and from other Arab governments and still supports Al-Jazeera. If this comes at the expense of Qatari news, then that will do, that's the price we're willing to pay." (al-Alami 2005) Al-Jazeera representatives have also repeatedly alleged that Al-Jazeera treats issues relative to Qatar equally when deemed newsworthy. (el-Nawawy and Iskandar 2002; Ballout 2005; Gaballah 2005; Khader 2005) The station has notably provided reports criticizing the Emir, the situation of women and expatriates in Qatar, the instrumentalization of religion as a means to exert social control, the presence of American troops on Qatari soil as well as the role of Qatar in the war on Iraq.

Devoted almost exclusively to news coverage and analysis, Al-Jazeera has steadily earned viewer loyalty from an estimated at 40 to 50 million in the Middle East, North Africa, and worldwide. (Ballout 2005) Yet bloody footage of war and the platform provided to political and religious dissidents also garnered both support as well as criticism of sensationalism and bias toward fundamentalists and extremist groups. (Ajami 2001; Fandy 2003; Fandy 2004; Hirst 2000a, 2000b) In the week of 29 March 2003 marking the start of the US-led war on Iraq, Al-Jazeera's official website (www.aljazeera.net) rose to the number 1 spot on Lycos 50's top 50 web search service.

(Lycos 50 2003) Al-Jazeera has released interviews with America's most wanted man, Osama bin Laden, but also videos produced by militant groups featuring prepared statements, pleas by their captives as well as missile launch footage. The channel has defended this editorial choice by arguing that this material is newsworthy. (Ballout 2005; Gaballah 2005; Khader 2005; Sheikh 2005) Furthermore, Al-Jazeera's talk shows have at times criticized militant activities. In a memorable July 7, 2001 episode of *Al-Ittijah al-Muakiss* (The Opposite Direction) on "Bin Laden, Arab despair and American fear," host Faisal al-Qasim refers in the program's introduction to bin Laden as *sheikh* bin Laden, a sign of respect toward tribal and/or religious status. Al-Qasim also begins with a passionate, lengthy account of the "Arab street's" praise of Bin Laden as a heroic underdog. Yet in balancing such content with live broadcasts and interviews of the war on terror's main proponents, the channel follows its policy "to provide a platform for both sides of an argument and leave viewers to make up their own minds," (Sakr 2002: 829) despite the inevitable criticism received from affected parties.

The channel introduced an entirely new format on 16 June 2005, including daily programs such as the 2-hour long news bulletins *Al-Jazeera Hazha as-Sabah* (Al-Jazeera this Morning – broadcast at 8 AM Mekka time), which also focuses on non-breaking news, and *Al-Jazeera Muntassif al-Yawm* (Al-Jazeera this Afternoon – broadcast at 4 PM Mekka time); and *Ma Wara' al-Khabar* (What's Behind the News – broadcast at 6.30 PM Mekka time), a political analysis program. In addition to shortening its weekly talk shows from 80 minutes to 55 minutes (not including commercial and news breaks) and introducing several new socio-cultural and political programs, the channel toned down its trailers, the introduction music accompanying its programs and its graphics in a move reflecting modernization and a less aggressive feel. Seeking to cover a broader range of subjects, Al-Jazeera's "future direction will be to reach the human as a human, with a human's hopes, pains and aspirations," announced Ahmed al-Sheikh in the station's first report from its new newsroom in Doha. The report's author, Mohammed Fal, also posited that "the humanitarian issues will [...] be the focus of Al-Jazeera now," a position demonstrated soon thereafter through the channel's subsequent focus on the crisis in Sudan's Darfur province and the Niger famine.

2. Creating a Public Space for Dialogue

Al-Jazeera's editorial policy has arguably helped foster a public space for dialogue and an alternative to other media outlets, such as the BBC, Radio Monte-Carlo, CNN, and the Arab government channels most prevalent in the Arab Middle East and North Africa before Al-Jazeera's inception. The channel's policy of presenting the various sides of an issue, however, poses a fundamental challenge as the channel does not maintain a permanent frame or enemy although reflecting and giving more weight to Arab opinions. Al-Jazeera's controversies have arguably increased its credibility and popularity among its audiences. Al-Arabiya, founded in February 2003 to provide a more moderate alternative, for example, has yet to gain as large a slice of the audience share (see Table 2. Arab Media Preferences). "Al-Jazeera is the most-watched Arab satellite station," argues Palestinian journalist and researcher Daoud Kuttab, "partly because its journalism is highly professional and partly because viewers like the fact that its reporters and anchors give the news a pro-Arab spin." (Kuttab 2003: 45)

The channel's audience is not limited to Arabic speakers living in Arab countries, but also comprises members of the "Arab diaspora"—displaced persons of Arab background (see Anderson 1995). As an Arabic-language satellite broadcaster, Al-Jazeera is inherently transnational and caters to collective identities spread across the globe, (Sakr 2001) such as Arabic-speakers, Arab nationals, and Muslims, the latter most emblematically portrayed by the weekly *Ash-Shari'a wal-Haya* (Islamic Law and Life) program. (Lamloun 2004) While the satellite television medium allows the channel to reach across and beyond borders, the easily recognizable *fus'ha* (formal Arabic) spoken by news anchors and program presenters also helps foster a sense of virtual community for Arabic speakers

13

of various backgrounds, in what Alterman terms a "new Arabism" as "Arabs' increasing interaction with non-Arab cultures, and their treatment by those cultures as Arabs rather than as holders of specific nationalities, moves Egyptians, Syrians, Palestinians, and Saudi Arabians to have a heightened Arab identity vis-à-vis the outside world." (Alterman 1999) The channel also at times cultivates dialogue between Arab and non-Arab views. As other media networks line up to purchase footage from Al-Jazeera, the channel effectively reverses the flow of information, posited by media imperialism theory as traditionally emanating from the "West" or "North." (See Schiller 1969, 1976, and 1996) Cultural imperialists further stress the tendency of Western, and especially Anglo-Saxon interests to dominate the global media market. (Comor 1997; Curran and Park 2000) However, this theoretical framework assumes a one-way flow of communication, much undermined by new technologies of communication, such as satellite broadcasting. A same material may provide differentiated responses depending, for example, on belief systems or cultural references.

Al-Jazeera provides an alternative source of information within an international news sphere typically dominated by Western media. However, "much like any other mass media outlet, Al-Jazeera creates a representation of reality, contextualizes facts, suggests links, renders the event coherent and comprehensive." (Lamloun 2004: 13) As a news outlet broadcasting out of the Arab world in Arabic and targeting Arabic speakers worldwide, the channel reflects a pan-Arab comprehension of current events. When this interpretation has clashed with those of governments and dominant news media, the channel has come under fierce attack. Yet Al-Jazeera's status as the Middle East's first free news network is significant in a context where much of the media have functioned under strict censorship and government control. (Sakr 2001) Olfa Lamloun suggests that the channel's role resides in creating a space that allows for the growth of an alternative political culture in the Arab world.

(Lamloun 2004) Rather than present a singular voice, Al-Jazeera reflects the multiplicity of an Arab world riveted by political, social, economic and religious differences. A mere glance into the newsroom reveals a core editorial team representing almost every Arab nationality and reflecting a wide spectrum of political leanings, from communism to moderate politics to Islamic fundamentalism. Souag acknowledges that "of course, there is no objectivity in the media," but insists "th[is] should never go over the limit of providing a platform." (Souag 2004) Ballout further opines that "in a sense, [the channel] has created a momentum within Arab societies and has perhaps led to a renewed belief in the power of civil societies, or a rediscovery of the potential in the role of a civil society, but not to mobilize" civil society. (Ballout 2005) Although shaped by pressures of its own, Al-Jazeera may then have provided a platform for discussion.

As posited by Senior Producer Samir Khader, "you can't wage a war without news, without media, without propaganda." (In Noujaim 2004) Although maintaining professional standards of news reporting, particularly in its news bulletins, a strong pro-Arab slant becomes apparent "in the editing and framing of stories, the angling of interviewers' questions, and the choice of sound and imagery for the dramatic plug spots that fill time between programs [*sic.*]" (Economist 2005) A promotional trailer for the weekly *Al-Mashad al-Iraqi* (The Iraqi Scene) played an emotional pitch with sentimental music and a flickering picture of a people toiling under occupation, caught between hope and despair. While allowing for the expression of opposing viewpoints, the channel tends to highlight the "plight" of Arab populations caused by external encroachment, particularly in its talk shows. In this sense, Al-Jazeera does not differ from other media in terms of its socio-political and cultural specificity. Just as the BBC and NPR originally emerged as efforts of the British and American foreign services, respectively, so Al-Jazeera, as a channel initiated by Arab efforts, reflects Arab concerns.

The following section examines different elements of the channel's discourse in more depth by applying a framing, or discourse analysis to weekly program episodes over a set time period. A proven research method in communications and media research, this approach, here explicitly applied to Al-Jazeera for the first time, framing analysis provides further insight into the means by which the channel has "toed the red lines."

Olivia Qusaibaty

3. *Application of a Framing/Discourse Analysis to Select Program Episodes*

The news media scrutinize events and assert their specificity through chronological and spatial differentiation. As social scientist Michel Foucault indicates, "It's not a matter of locating everything on one level, that of the event, but of realizing that there is actually a whole order of levels of different types of events differing in amplitude, chronological breadth, and capacity to produce effects." (Foucault 1980: 114) Analyzing the ways in which the media frame particular events or topics therefore requires determining the degree to which they present these same events or topics in a holistic fashion, or otherwise. The framing analysis introduced here attempts to empirically test the thesis central to the research presented in this paper and the posited Al-Jazeera "opinion and the other opinion" media model: Al-Jazeera's ability to provide an alternative news source (to other Western and Arab news outlets) and to create a public space for dialogue free of censorship or control. This additional research therefore serves to reveal patterns in Al-Jazeera's attempts to satisfy its own media model through its dialectical approach to news framing and analysis. The January and March 2005 episodes (7-8 per program) of three different weekly programs: *Al-Ittijah al-Muakiss* (The Opposite Directions), *Hiwar Maftouh* (Open Discussion) and *Lil-Nissa' Faqat* (For Women Only)[2], were

---

[2] The episodes analysed for all three programs lasted an average of 80 minutes, with a brief 5-6 minutes news bulletin on the hour and 1 to 2-minute long commercial breaks spread throughout the program. During the first 5 to 10 minutes, the host presents the topic and issues at hand as well as the featured guests. The last 15 to 30 minutes of Lil-Nissa' Faqat and Al-Ittijah al-Muakiss are open to the public, who present their comments either live by telephone or in writing by email or fax simile. Each Al-Ittijah al-Muakiss episode also features a single yes/no question to which the

watched a first time live and again during either the second or third broadcast on Al-Jazeera. Subsequently, the written and audio transcripts were obtained from the channel's broadcasting website, www.aljazeera.net/channel (see Lil-Nissa' Faqat 2005; Al-Ittijah al-Muakiss 2005; Hiwar Maftouh 2005; Table 5. Selection of Al-Jazeera Programs for Framing Analysis). These three programs were chosen over the four other primetime weekly live programs (broadcast at 9.35 PM Mekka time before June 2005 and at 10.05 PM Mekka time thereafter) in order to delimit the analysis and examine programs that differ notably in the topics addressed and presentation style.

Presented by Louna ash-Shebl, Lil-Nissa' Faqat has aired as an ongoing weekly feature with three or more guests per episode until June 2005, following the channel's second major change of layout and programming. The most infamous and controversial talk-show program on Al-Jazeera, Al-Ittijah al-Muakiss is hosted by Syrian journalist Faisal al-Qasim and operates on the same principle as CNN's "Crossfire." Political commentators and dissidents representing opposing ends of a same issue meet on the channel's platform for an often-heated debate on contemporary issues. In contrast to Al-Ittijah al-Muakiss in particular, Hiwar Maftouh, hosted by Ghassan bin Jeddo, tends to feature more moderate guests and a more balanced debate, thanks in part to its format, which comprises a small studio audience invited to question the guests and host. A sample of Al-Jazeera's talk shows was chosen over recorded programs or news bulletins as it is through these that "the Arab population [began] to hear, on the air, a new kind of discourse" (Bahry 2001: 103) that challenged that of the previously

---

audience can either respond via the Al-Jazeera website, email, telephone, or facsimile. Al-Qasim provides updates of the poll throughout the episode. Hiwar Maftouh episodes featured a live audience, whose members usually participated in the second segment of the show, after the news bulletin. The first broadcast of every program is aired live.

prevalent government-controlled channels and offered an alternative to their Western equivalents.

Observing episodes from two non-consecutive months enables assessment of discourse on a greater variety of issues. However, this choice places inherent limitations on the research. The conclusions drawn from this analysis therefore do not necessarily apply to the channel's programming as a whole. Table 4. Main Live and Recorded Al-Jazeera Programs provides details on a selection of other programs broadcast on the channel. Framing, or discourse, analysis has been chosen over a content analysis as the categorization and allocation of words implicated in the latter remains normative, as the researcher delimits the different categories and chooses which words fit into which categories. In addition, those words absent from reports may also provide insight into a channel's coverage. This work seeks instead to determine the channel's framing of issues and events, most evident in programs prepared by policy-makers in the organization, (see Entman 1993, 1989) such as talk shows. A proven research method, framing analysis determines how the media frame events or issues, and assumes that the choice of words reflects opinions. This method underlines

> "attempts to close meaning down, to fix it in relation to a given position, to make certain conversations self-evidently correct, to do creative repair work when something becomes problematic, and to make the subject positions of discourse transparently obvious, without any viable alternatives." (Deacon *et al.* 1999: 154)

As suggested by Deacon, the analysis here attempts to uncover cues for social experience (knowledge and beliefs), relational discourse ("I" versus "you," "we" and "they") and aspects of social reality raised in the episodes. Framing will be evaluated horizontally by addressing the main ideas conveyed, the paradigmatic structure—or vertical set of elements chosen by the actors—, the speakers chosen and a semantic (syntagmatic)—the horizontal chain in which elements are linked with one another according to agreed codes and conventions—analysis. Three methods can therein be deployed: focus groups, a cumulative model and an impulse model (see Deacon *et al.* 1999). The cumulative model, adopted here in order to facilitate the analytical process and eliminate the external variables prevalent in the other two models, gathers data over a set period of time, i.e. the January and March 2005 episodes of three select programs.

A framing analysis of the various program episodes revealed certain patterns in the approach and framing of various issues. A constant juxtaposition and differentiation between the "West and the rest," or more precisely, "the West and the Arab world" appears throughout. This dichotomy presents itself in several different ways, including what may be termed paranoia of Western socio-political and economic "invasion," a battle tone, a framing of problems as emerging from the West, globalization and the United States termed as "external forces," and a very definite focus on the United States when addressing "Western" issues. Often imposing his or her own subjective framing and interrupting guests in order to influence the direction of the discussion, the program host also often reinforced the anti-Western sentiment expressed by guests and callers, and at times provided dubious information.

Dichotomous analysis
American or European efforts to alleviate challenges facing the Arab world, including human rights issues, are at times framed as cultural invasions, whose purpose is to "destroy" Arab identities. In the 1 March episode of Al-Ittijah al-Muakiss on police states and Syria and Lebanon, Al-Qasim frames the events surrounding the upcoming pullout of Syrian troops (posted in Lebanon since the beginning of the country's civil war) by asserting that "it is obvious that there are large scale plans by Israel and the US to control the region. Syria is following Iraq." The host also referred to the "fact" that "we [Arabs] are tooled [...] The Americans pretend that they are against dictatorships and police states, but the facts reveal

otherwise." Referring to the March 2005 Commission on the Status of Women (Beijing + 10) conference held in New York, Mothana al-Kurdistany, a caller on the Lil-Nissa' Faqat 7 March episode suggests that "we do not want an arrogant, dominant, Western culture. We do not want to be in a position where we a receiving the Western culture as a consumer market." Anything emerging from the West is framed as exploitative, and leading to the loss of socio-political and economic independence. On the same episode and referring to women's rights, guest Aza al-Hur Marwa contends that "we are facing challenges that are designed to destroy our Arabic identity, our Arab culture. [...] My Arab identity is here on the line, my Arab culture is on the line, my Arab civilization is on the line." A The 28 March episode of *Lil-Nissa' Faqat*, which focuses on the difficulties of Western Muslim women, presents another notable example of dichotomous discourse. In discussing Western women's conversion to Islam, the host assumes that they have converted from Christianity to Islam, despite the religious plurality of the populations of Western Europe and the United States (where one might convert from Judaism, Buddhism or others to Islam).

In the 11 January *Al-Ittijah al-Muakiss* episode, al-Qasim calls the Iraqi elections "an American pre-cooked meal" and a "historical crime," arguing that "the elections were fabricated according to the Israeli way in order to legitimize the occupation [of Iraq] and give authority to people who have no legitimacy." Like most of his program introductions, al-Qasim here chooses to deliver a highly emotional commentary: "Do they think that these people who came to Iraq in tanks and destroyed entire cities and killed thousands of people and planted mass graves everywhere and stole even the statues from the streets and the museums, do they think that the Iraqi people will accept a ruler for Iraq through an election that is fake from head to toe?" The host also adopts a defeatist mentality, namely suggesting that "isn't it true that all the Iraqi elections are a joke anyways? So why would we be upset about another joke?" Louna ash-Shebl recognizes in the 31 January episode on the sexual exploitation of children that "we are always accusing the West of being socially disjointed, governed with no ethics or morality." (Lil-Nissa' Faqat) She then asks guests to shift their focus on the Arab world. Guest Sourour Quarouni interjects by arguing that the problems, here the sexual exploitation of children, are universal.

Hiwar Maftouh episodes presented a more moderate debate. Host Ghassan bin Jeddo, who also serves as Al-Jazeera's Beirut bureau chief, namely offered in his introductions a comprehensive historical overview of the events behind the issues to be discussed. In the 15th January episode on political tension in Lebanon for example, bin Jeddo begins by highlighting the socio-political scene in Lebanon, asking "we open the cave of Ali Baba and what do we find?," and focusing on the development of the opposition, most of whose constituents do not see signs of a *coup d'état* despite the "police order" in Lebanon and signs of political unrest in light of the "question of the Syrian military" in Lebanon and pressure from UN Resolution 1559, which calls for a withdrawal of all Syrian troops in the country and the disarmament of armed militias, such as the Shiite faction Hezbollah. Throughout the discussion, bin Jeddo manages to prevent the discussion from escalating between the two main guests, Michel Aoun and Ali Hassan al-Khalil. Although reverential toward Aoun, leader of the Free Patriotic Movement and then-exiled former military leader, the host nevertheless does not hesitate to interrupt him in order to request clarification (e.g. as to whom amongst the opposition Aoun believes is interested in gaining political control) or to allow some of the university students invited on the show's platform to speak. When two of the audience members debate on a side issue – the border dispute with Israel in South Lebanon – bin Jeddo allows them engage in a discussion for a short period of time before re-orienting the discussion so that the student addresses his question directly to one of the two featured guests.

Talk about the West focuses almost exclusively on the United States

When introducing "the West," the discussion at times adopted a battle tone and referred almost exclusively to the United States, framed as *al-quwa al-kharijiya* (the external force). In the 7 March and 11 January episodes of Lil-Nissa' Faqat in particular, globalization is also seen as termed universally by an "external force." The hosts also attempted to introduce America or Israel as major players responsible for socio-political and economic difficulties in the Arab world. Al-Jazeera New York correspondent Abd al-Rahim Fouqara's report featured in the 7 March episode of *Lil-Nissa' Faqat* refers almost exclusively to the American position at New York conference. Fouqara' argues that the event focused solely on the issue of the right to abortion, introduced as particularly sensitive to American representatives. Program guest Maha Abu Diya Shamas similarly argues that "the conflict between the United States and the other nation-states in the world took a whole week wasting the precious time of those who came to New York." The US, termed broadly by hosts and guests, is therefore seen as a major reason for the lack of development on issues of concern.

Ironically enough, despite their unrelenting criticism of the "West," guests, and at times, the host, replicated English terminology, framed events focusing on the American in particular, and European viewpoint, and situated their arguments in reference to largely Anglo-Saxon frameworks. All statistics related to the sexual education of children provided in the 31 January episode of Lil-Nissa' Faqat referred to the particular situation in the United States. In the 17 January episode focusing on the sexual exploitation of children, most of the statistics used in the discussion addressed child abuse and sexual molestation in the United States. The single reference to statistics concerning the Arab world alleges that some studies, which were not referenced, indicate that 75% of rape cases for children and women in the Arab world occur within the family or are committed by persons close to the family or victim.

In the 18 January episode of Al-Ittijah al-Muakiss, al-Qasim asks guest Ghazi Suleiman, "despite the historical importance of this [Nairobi peace] agreement [for Sudan], don't you think that it is concealing a dangerous matter, which is the possibility of dividing Sudan into two separate states, which is an American policy in the region to separate the Arab world into smaller states for minorities?" The 9 January 2005 Nairobi agreement does indeed grant autonomy to Sudan's Southern region for six years, to be followed by a referendum on independence. However, al-Qasim attempts to apply his reasoning of America's negative involvement to other ethno-social strife issues in the region, such as those concerning the Iraqi Kurds, the Iraqi Shiites, and the possibility of dividing Saudi Arabia into smaller states.

Subjective framing

Each *Al-Ittijah al-Muakiss* episode features a poll on a specific question open to all who visit the Al-Jazeera website, e-mail, or call in their response. However, these questions tend to reveal a strong accusatory tone. For the 4 January episode, Al-Qasim asked his audience, "Do you think that America and Israel are responsible for delaying development in the Arab world?" This question encourages the respondent to answer "yes," as it does not offer any other options as to the causes for delayed development in the Arab world and already assumes that some entity is responsible. The fact that *Al-Ittijah al-Muakiss* questions require a "yes" or "no" response may help explain the inherent limitations they impose on the respondents. Throughout his belligerent introductions, Al-Qasim paints an overly negative image of America and Israel's intervention in development in the Arab world. In the January 4 episode on the

Olivia Qusaibaty

UN Arab Human Development Reports, al-Qasim infers, "didn't [the Americans] use the conclusions of this report as justification for invading Iraq and explicitly interfering with Arab affairs on the pretext that Arabs are incapable of advancing themselves and controlling themselves?" The sole attempt at "balance" or "objectivity" is usually presented at the end of the introduction, such as when he states that "we [Arabs] should stop blaming the outside variables for development problems in the Arab world." (4 January) However, "the other direction" is demised as the host has already endorsed opposition to "the Americans." Al-Qasim has been criticized for adopting prior notions that he pushes forward in the form of a discussion or dialog. (Al-Shammari 1998, 1999; Al-Zaidi 2003) However, al-Qasim has argued that he believes in the need to engage the Arab intelligentsia on a global level for arguments on controversial issues such as nationalism, communism and Zionism. (Al-Zaidi 2003; Al-Kasim 2005; Bahry 2001)

During the 24 January episode of Lil-Nissa' Faqat, which focuses on the work of voluntary organizations for women, host and guests (mainly Ikhbar Loghan) insist that while the US has often pledged aid for international development and crises, it rarely provided the actual funds. A video segment features then US Secretary of State Colin Powell announcing that the United States will respond to the Southeast Asian tsunami disaster because of the humanitarian aspect of this crisis. He also posits that while most of these countries are Islamic countries, the US will act regardless of religion, thereby providing the Islamic world and the rest of the world "an opportunity to see the American generosity and the American values on the ground, since we value the dignity of individuals, and our response is to satisfy this dignity, regardless of religion." The decision to present this video segment may reflect an attempt to frame American relations with the Islamic world as based upon religion and dominance, and America as antagonistic to Islam. Throughout the discussion, different speakers posit that the penultimate US conflict with the Arab world, The Global War on Terror, affects civil donations negatively as Islamic countries have since placed constraints on civil organizations out of fear of terrorism. Amany Qandyl suggests that charity organizations were most affected in the countries that American Congress representatives visited after September 11 because of the restrictions imposed on donations and collections "under the pretext of counter-terrorism." The War on Terror, as framed by US policymakers, is therefore seen to impede the pursuit and progress of volunteer work.

Following the viewing of a speech by US President George W. Bush in this same episode, Louna ash-Shebl asks one of the guests to make a comment on both video clips, particularly Bush's speech. She immediately mentions to keep in mind the fact that US Secretary of Defense Donald Rumsfeld stands to the right of the president, discussing the help that came from the military, "as though the soldiers in this military institution are not occupying Iraq. They are people who are bombing and shelling us." The host therefore frames any potential response and also contributes to a sense of a collective identity that is under attack, since the US military is "bombing and shelling us." Iqbar Doghan replies by suggesting that only a small portion of the West's promised aid in the past has actually reached those in need and that this aid mostly served propaganda purposes. As with Al-Qasim and bin Jeddo, Ash-Shebl does not challenge the figures provided nor request references, but rather simply summarizes the guest's points. The hosts also tended not to provide references for their own commentary. In Al-Ittijah al-Muakiss's 1 March episode, Al-Qasim claims that there is "no doubt that Syria is targeted, even the American press talked about it, that since 1996 there is a plan. Three Israeli officials in Europe were trying to build public opinion against Syria." The host does not specify which paper(s) or magazine(s) he spoke of nor which Israeli officials participated in the alleged plan against Syria.

Olivia Qusaibaty

In a number of Al-Ittijah al-Muakiss episodes, al-Qasim states speculations as facts. In the 4 January episode for example, he blatantly misinforms the audience by stating that the UNDP Arab Human Development Report is forbidden from publication and circulation, whereas it is actually available for download on the UN website (see UNDP 2005). In the same episode, al-Qasim alleges that the Arab Human Development has been banned, yet he provides no evidence apart from a comment by chief author Nader al-Farjani—who indicated that America and Israel were responsible for the delay of human development in the Arab world—that the report was published and then banned (the report was published three months later, in April 2005). (Saleh 2004)

The host interrupts the speaker and influences the discussion's orientation
In a number of Lil-Nissa' Faqat episodes, the host interjects during a guest of caller's exposé, usually in order to influence the direction of subsequent discussion. While a host's role consists in channeling and managing a discussion, this role is impeded when the host imposes or reinforces a particular viewpoint. The most notable example emerges from the 3 January episode on future potential diseases for survivors of the December 2004 South East Asia Tsunami, hosted by Fairuz Zayani. While the host managed to instigate dialogue between the guests in an orderly fashion, she interrupted different speakers on several occasions, finishing off their sentences. This anticipation of speakers' ensuing comments may affect the dialogue's future direction.

While Ghassan bin Jeddo also interrupted his guests on several occasions, he did so in order to allow another guest to speak or introduce a different aspect of the issue (see Hiwar Maftouh 2005). Faisal Al-Qasim, who has explicitly referred to his program as "a rooster fight," (Al-Afandy 2002) does adopt a rather disrespectful attitude toward some of his guests, which

27

may seem evidence of lack of journalistic integrity. In the 4 January episode, guest Manir Shafiq says "don't tell me about interests. America and Israel are enemies. I mean, the imperialist America is not just an enemy of the Arabs, it's an enemy of..." Al-Qasim completes the sentence with "...of humanity," while Shafiq continues with "...for most of the world. And this feeling is not just limited to Arabs. It's an international issue, and the problem of this report is that it demonstrates the Arab problem, but this is really a third world problem." Not only did Al-Qasim encourage Shafiq to continue to unabashedly make allegations against the US and the Arab world, he also let the discussion drift away from that episode's central theme, the Arab Human Development Report 2004. In this same episode, which was broadcast 3 months before the publication of the report, another example of framing on the part of the host may be found in his exchange with guest Nadil Fayad below:

Fayad: The report will be published. Let's wait for it and see what it says. We are talking about a report that has not yet been published.

Al-Qasim: Wait for what? It's already forbidden.

Fayad: It's not forbidden. It's going to be published soon.

Al-Qasim: Published after three quarters of it will be removed.

Fayad: How could you assume something you don't know?

The host continuously incites his guests and argues with them in order to impose a particular point of view, which is also demonstrated by his physical gesturing (shaking arms and hands vertically). Another example of Al-Qasim's attempts to frame the discussion in certain ways lies in his description of and interaction with the guests. In the 18 January episode on Sudan's Nairobi peace agreement, he presents guest Ghazi Suleiman, Chairman of the National Coalition to Restore Democracy in Sudan, as "overly optimistic" and engages in a person-to-person debate with him, therein lending much less airtime to the other guest, Hassan Saty.

Olivia Qusaibaty

Attempts at resolving differences
While most Al-Ittijah al-Muakiss episodes often closely resemble shouting matches, al-Qasim does at times attempt to bring more calm to the discussion when the two guests drift too far away from the central issues, such as in the 11 January episode on the Iraqi elections. For much of the episode, both guests engage in personal allegations and criticism. While Khalaf Abd as-Samd argues that "we need to keep the discussion at a higher lever, we can't vilify everyone," Nouri al-Mouradi refuses to tone down his commentary, namely positing that "what I'm going to say to the American people is, whether the elections happen in Iraq or not, the liberation of Iraq will occur through resistance, whether you like it or not." When the discussion degrades into personal allegations, al-Qasim attempts to bring the discussion back to the main topic, but with little initial success and much frustration. Unlike Al-Ittijah al-Muakiss and Lil-Nissa' Faqat, Hiwar Maftouh episodes presented a more balanced discussion, where the host attempted and succeeded in allotting almost equal attention to the different opinions voiced. Bin Jeddo does not take sides and does not put forth his own opinion in obvious ways but rather plays a strong mediator role between the different parties.

Critics point to the tendency of Al-Ittijah al-Muakiss to deliberately bring diametrically opposed speakers. (Al-Shammari 1998, 1999; Bahry 2001) Verbal exchange often escalates to fighting words. The program illustrates an example of infotainment—entertainment packaged as news (Mohammadi 1998)—while creating division and provocation, (al-Zaidi 2003) rather than a more neutral dialogue such as that found in Hiwar Maftouh. Lil-Nissa' Faqat, which broke new ground by focusing on taboo topics affecting the daily life of women in the Arab world, tended to develop a dichotomous discourse, though not as polarized as that of Al-Ittijah al-Muakiss. These and other weekly programs such as *Ash-Shari'ah wal-Haya* have shaken the Arab world by tackling issues sensitive to Muslims and Arabs broadcast live, and therefore devoid of manifest censorship. (Miles 2005) As demonstrated through the framing analysis, these shows have a tendency for sensationalism while presenters press for emotions and arguments amongst the panelists. Through such often emotionally charged programs, one may question Al-Jazeera's neutrality, as do some of the program guests. In the 11 January episode of Al-Ittijah al-Muakiss, Khalaf Abd as-Samd, a guest representing a more moderate view on the Iraqi elections issue, questions the accuracy of the show's voting process, as throughout the episode an overwhelming majority (varying between 70% and 79%) of respondents responded "no" to the featured question, "do you think that the elections support the Iraqis in light of the occupation?" Presenting initial voting results at the beginning of each episode "frames" the ensuing responses (viewers are encouraged to keep voting during the show). Presenting the vote results only at the end of the show would help prevent clustering of the votes. Abd as-Samd sarcastically comments "thank you for this type of honest media," perhaps out of anger, feeling that his point was not properly taken into consideration.

In Al-Jazeera's attempt to satisfy its two core objectives of providing an alternative news medium and creating a public space of dialogue free from control and censorship, the channel was led to use "the opinion and the other opinion" as its quintessential model. Based on the analysis above, the channel's actual application of this model is rife with controversy. While a news channel is expected to report facts, Al-Jazeera's talk shows do just the opposite by airing only opinions and at times reporting opinions as facts. Furthermore, by framing the issues of those appearing on its platform, these talk shows abused the freedom of endowed to the channel. By selectively endorsing some opinions and ignoring others and by sometimes imposing its own editorial line, Al-Jazeera does not act as a mediator between several voices but rather violates basic journalistic credibility and objectivity, in complete

Olivia Qusaibaty

violation of its own code of ethics (see Document 1. Al-Jazeera Code of Ethics). Despite the consistency of the patterns identified above, one should consider the broader context, beyond the specific programs and dates. In abiding to its motto, the opinion and the other opinion, Al-Jazeera has tended to offer a dichotomous view of world happenings, caught between one extreme and the other, and most often involving the mediation of violence. In choosing to focus discussion within this context, the West has come under sharp criticism on Al-Jazeera's airwaves. The channel has nevertheless repeatedly presented strong condemnation of the abuses of Arab and other regimes. (Al-Zaidi 2003)

4. Paying the Price for Critical Coverage

While Arab governments and audiences criticized the channel from the outset, it was at first praised in Europe and North America for encouraging free speech in the Arab world. As London Bureau Chief Mostefa Souag suggests, "the West at first welcomed this fresh, new voice." (Souag 2004) The US State Department Report in 2000 highlighted that the channel is "privately owned," "operates freely" and has criticized the government's attempts at normalization with Israel. (U.S. Department of State 2000) In this first phase however, Al-Jazeera reported the destructive aspects of Saddam Hussein's regime to his people, the same conditions upon which the US administration rested justification to go to war. The channel's subsequent emphasis on the human cost of war during the second Intifada (2000-2005), but especially of the wars in Afghanistan (2001) and Iraq (2003 and ensuing conflict), which were backed by US-led coalition forces, drew fierce criticism, more particularly in the United States and to a lesser extent in the United Kingdom. Al-Jazeera has faced much criticism from Arab governments—most notably Saudi Arabia, Kuwait, Bahrain, Jordan, Palestinian Authority, Libya, Tunisia, where it has been banned—accused namely of bias toward Islam or Iraq, and as an American front and device to normalize relations with Israel. (Ghareeb 2001) In May 2005, the Egyptian government briefly detained 8 Al-Jazeera journalists in order to prevent them from covering a general assembly meeting of the Cairo Judges' Club deciding on the future of the Egyptian constitution. The Moroccan government detained Al-Jazeera's correspondent there following his coverage of the political tension in Western Sahara in July 2005. The channel's crew received a harsher response in Yemen when the government detained Al-Jazeera cameramen and a correspondent there following the channel's exclusive coverage of the July 2005 riots in Sana'a against the government subsidies on food and oil. In response to Al-Jazeera and Al-Arabiya's outspoken criticism of the former Iraqi Council members and Coalition "forces of the occupation," the US-backed Iraqi Interim government withdrew the both channels' rights to report on official government activities, later followed by an official ban on its operations.

Airing virtually uncensored recordings and interviews with political and religious dissidents, including Osama bin Laden, also led to accusations of strong bias. (Ajami 2001; Fandy 2003; Fandy 2004) Al-Jazeera stumbled into Americans' living rooms on 7 October 2001, the day British and American forces began their campaign against the Taliban and its supporters in Afghanistan, with an exclusive interview with Osama bin Laden, head of the Al-Qaeda terrorist organization the US government sought to neutralize for terrorist activities in Afghanistan and elsewhere. In the interview, bin Laden commends the 11 September 2001 attacks carried out against the United States. Numerous television stations simultaneously broadcast Al-Jazeera's interview, mirroring a similar move during "Operation Desert Fox" in 1998, where the channel's footage of the Iraq War was rebroadcast on US networks. (Gaballah 2005) Al-Jazeera's bin Laden exclusive led US State Department spokesman Richard Boucher to claim that al-Qaeda and Al-Jazeera are "bound by a common hatred" (USInfo 2003) while US Defense Secretary Donald Rumsfeld advanced that Arab media such as Al-Jazeera and Al Arabiya "have persuaded an enormous fraction" of people that the United States is an occupation force in Iraq and that U.S. soldiers "are randomly killing innocent civilians, which is a lie." (USInfo 2004) However, it was US-based ABC News channel and not Al-Jazeera that first broadcast an exclusive interview with the terror mastermind in May 1998. (Miller 1998)

A one-month ban beginning in January 28, 2004 was applied to Al-Jazeera following an episode of Al-Ittijah al-Muakiss on "Israel's infiltration in Iraq." Featuring guests Dr. Nouri al-Mouradi, the Iraqi Communist Party spokesman, and Hamid al-Kafaiee, the Iraqi Governing Council spokesman, the discussion focused on such issues as "Israel's ambitions in Iraq, accusations directed against some Iraqi political leaders of spying in favor of Israel and the role of Israel in the invasion of Iraq." Al-Mouradi notably alleged that Israel had infiltrated Iraq, including through cooperation between Israeli and Kurdish leaders dating back to 1968. Claiming that the channel presented a negative image of Iraq and encouraged anti-Coalition sentiment, the Allawi administration shut down Al-Jazeera's Iraq office on August 7, 2004 for "inciting violence and hatred." (Allawi in Mroue 2004) On September 4, 2004, Iraq extended the ban indefinitely. Ballout argued that the channel both abided by the temporary ban and used agency footage of events unraveling in Iraq, adding that "we [Al-Jazeera] have never compromised our editorial values. We believe that what happens in Iraq is very important for the whole Arab world and needs to be covered comprehensively, objectively and in a balanced way." (in Harding 2004) The channel's coverage at the time stood out from many other media outlets. As former American Lieutenant Josh Rushing of the Al-Udeid base in Qatar explained, "the night they showed the P.O.W.'s and dead soldiers, it was powerful, because Americans won't show those kinds of images," (in Noujaim 2004) coverage for which US Defense Secretary Donald Rumsfeld accused the channel of breaching the Geneva Conventions. During the Iraq War in particular, and to a far lesser extent during the continuing violence that has torn the country, the channel lent particular focus to the plight of civilians "under the American occupation." Through non-affiliated journalists on the ground and newswire footage, the channel has nevertheless continued to provide almost daily reporting of the events unraveling there. A weekly program launched during the Iraq War, *Al-Mashad al-Iraqi* offers in-depth coverage of civil, political and economic questions of concern in Iraq.

Al-Jazeera's controversies have also affected its finances. Largely due to its difficulty in securing advertising, Al-Jazeera continues to receive partial financial assistance from the Qatari government. According to spokesman Jihad Ballout, "the case of Al-Jazeera defies every business logic in the world. You have an average of 40 million viewers a day. One would think that providers of products and services would be queuing to advertise on our space. This never happened, simply because advertising spend in the Middle East is a function of politics, not of economics." He also argues that the channel "has been placed under a *de facto* economic embargo since day one—regional as well as international [...] Any money invested or spent on Al-Jazeera for advertising would be deemed to be financing a network that has been a maverick as a best case scenario and a disrupting factor by some people." (Ballout 2005) Nevertheless, advertising expenditures in the Arab world remain relatively low Total advertising expenditures in the region were estimated at 1,482 million USD in 2004, where television accounts for 89 percent of the market share per year. (PARC 2005) In contrast, the US advertising market registered a figure of 245,573 million USD in 2003, where cable television and broadcast television together account for 24.8 percent of the market. (NAA 2004) By choosing to systematically offer opinions and their opposites, the channel has reaped anger from interested parties that have threatened the channel's very activities.

5. Bowing to Pressure?

In attempting to provide "the opinion and the other opinion," the channel inevitably garners both criticism and praise for reflecting opinions and their opposites, thereby impeding its very capacity to abide by this editorial policy. Al-Jazeera has therein suffered a number of attacks, direct and otherwise, to its operations. In the tense pre-Iraq invasion atmosphere, the New York Stock Exchange banned Al-Jazeera along with several other undisclosed news organizations on the grounds of "security concerns" on March 24, 2003. (In AP 2003) The Nasdaq Stock Market revoked Al-Jazeera's press credentials two days later. A US missile destroyed the satellite channel's Kabul offices on November 13, 2001, while two US bombs were dropped on the news channel's Baghdad office April 8, 2003, killing reporter Tareq Ayyoub. That same day, coalition tanks fired on the Abu Dhabi TV office and the Palestine hotel, home to non-embedded reporters, causing the death of two journalists. On May 21st, 2004, Hamid Rashid Wali, an Iraqi technician working for Al-Jazeera, was killed during clashes between the US military and the Shiite militia of Moqtada al-Sadr. (IFJ 2004) US forces in Iraq have arrested and jailed more than 20 Al-Jazeera journalists. (Younge and Dood 2005) Al-Jazeera reporters Tayseer Allouni—the Al-Jazeera journalist made famous by his interview with Bin Laden after September 11th and exclusive reports from Afghanistan—and Diyar al-Omari were both at one stage banned from reporting in Iraq. Following an initial arrest in September 2003, Allouni was placed in solitary confinement in Madrid for 119 days from November 2004 through March 2005. (Reuters 2005; El-Menshawy and Assir 2005) Cameraman Sami al-Haj remains interned in the Guantanamo Bay prison. Yet Al-Jazeera was not the only media outlet targeted. In August 2004, for example, close to 60 journalists, including BBC, Guardian, Independent, Times and Telegraph reporters, were seized by Iraqi police and held at gunpoint. (Harding 2004) The enforcement of embedded journalism for media coverage of conflict areas in the Afghanistan and Iraq wars tempered potential criticism of Coalition activities. In the United States, the Patriot Act of 2001 and other pressures from the government to demonstrate "patriotism" led to the news media's self-censorship. The five major American news networks – ABC, CBS, CNN, Fox News and NBC – agreed to limit their prospective news coverage and to withhold from airing material deemed to incite violence against Americans following a conference call by former US National Security Adviser, Condoleezza Rice. (Carter and Barringer 2001: 1)

Recommendations from an 11 September 2003 report of a commission comprised of CIA, FBI, Pentagon, US Senate and US Congress members presented to the American President included issuing an urgent warning to the Qatari government requiring closure of the channel and an immediate change of the channel's internal structure by replacing current executives with more moderate figures. The American administration had also taken its criticism directly to the Qatari government, reflecting an association between the channel and the Gulf state adopted by numerous critics, namely denying Qatar an invitation to a Summer 2004 Middle East summit in Georgia. In a move that some characterized as bowing to pressure, (Bradley 2004) the channel implemented changes. In late November 2003, the channel appointed a new manager, a new board of directors and implemented some reorganization of staff following government orders. The Emir had called for the board to modernize the channel as well as "enhance the station's capabilities and ensure the standards of professionalism." (In Baatout 2003) Though mostly superficial, changes included switching posts for reporters and representatives, a more discrete logo, while the main news program, *Hassad al-Yawm* (Today's Harvest – hour-long, broadcast at 11 PM Mekka time), featured two journalists instead of one, several new cultural programs and documentaries on more mundane subjects were offered. The channel institutionalized its practices by publishing a code of ethics and a code of conduct. (Jazeera 2004; see Document 1. Al-Jazeera Code of Ethics) The June 2005 change of layout described earlier has not yet substantiated significant allegations of bowing to pressure. The channel's announcement on 31 January 2005 of privatization plans has also given rise to speculations of pressure from the Bush administration. (Weisman 2005) Ahmed Sheikh, the channel's editor-in chief, insists that "Al-Jazeera will not change its editorial policy. […] We cannot compromise our integrity, our impartiality or our editorial policy," (Sheikh 2005) a claim also endorsed by Jihad Ballout (see AFP 2005).

The channel has also garnered much criticism for airing the statements and opinions of government opposition—especially in its violent expressions—such as Islamist groups claiming responsibility for terrorist attacks or terrorist cells operating in Iraq. The station was also the first in the region to feature interviews with Israeli citizens and government representatives, fuelling suspicions and accusations that the channel supports the Zionist cause or is funded by Mossad, the Israeli secret service. (Al-Zaidi 2003) Political scientist Olfa Lamloun explains this seeming ambivalence as the channel's core feature: "pressured by the United States, financed and monitored by the Qatari government, the pan-Arab channel plays with and unravels the various hegemonic strategies. Since its very beginning, it reveals the breaches created by the [new] world disorder in the Arab world. It reports the increasing disequilibrium in the region." (Lamloun 2004: 9) Schleifer further argues that "it was Al Jazeera's talk shows and sometimes its reporting which more than any particular pan-Arab politician stirred anti-Americanism in the region, while Qatar built a military base [El-Udeid] to host the very US/Coalition Central Command that directed the invasion of

Iraq." (Schleifer 2004) The argument that the channel fuels anti-Americanism represents a main concern behind the US joint commission. If the messenger provides a "distorted" view, it must be silenced. As suggested by the results of a Zogby International May 2004 survey, anti-American sentiment is often seen to originate more from dissatisfaction with American policies in the Middle East than from possibly biased news. The survey found that more than 75 percent of respondents in the 6 countries surveyed based their attitudes toward the United States more on American policy in the Middle East than on American values (see Table 3. Sources of Attitudes Toward the US). Al-Jazeera has denied claims that it provides incendiary coverage. Rather, as Senior Producer for the channel Samir Khader puts forth in Jehane Noujaim's 2004 *Control Room* documentary, "Al-Jazeera's mission is "to educate the Arab masses [...] Wake up! Wake up! There is a world around you. You are still sleeping." (Khader in Noujaim 2004)

6. The Opinion and the Other Opinion?

Arab governments were the first to criticize and condemn Al-Jazeera. (Al-Nawawy and Iskandar 2002; Al-Zaidi 2003; Hirst 2000a, 2000b; Miles 2005) The channel's attempts to provide "the opinion and the other opinion" by notably allowing political and religious dissidents to speak on its platform has often turned against the broadcaster. An interview with a Hamas leader led to accusations from the Palestinian Authority, while both the Egyptian and Algerian governments reacted angrily to Islamic dissidents appearing on the channel and Manama to a Bahraini dissident's interview on the channel. Iran objected to the coverage it received, once successfully requesting the removal of a satirical cartoon on Al-Jazeera's website. Morocco, Tunisia and Libya have all at one time recalled their ambassadors from Qatar in response to criticism voiced on Al-Jazeera's airwaves. The Syrian government often alleged the channel was part of a Zionist plan to bring discord to the Arab world. Reflecting on these and other responses, former Al-Jazeera head of international relations, the late Maher Abdallah, noted that the channel's "offices have been closed in many an Arab capital before. The wording of the justification of such action may differ from one country to another, but the gist is always the same: undermining state security (normally code for criticizing the leadership); providing a platform for terrorists (usually means political opposition); and insulting the people of the country (normally means criticizing a failed policy)." (Abdallah 2004) Yet perhaps the best illustration of the shortcomings of the channel's abidance to its motto lies in Al-Ittijah al-Muakiss, one of the talk shows analyzed in chapter 3. As Bahry has argued, the program's host, Faisal al-Qasim at times voices harsh criticism of the American, Israeli, and Arab governments in order to bring excitement to the televised debate, but does not attempt to reconcile—the often personal—differences between the guests. Rather, al-Qasim "tries to provoke his guests as much as he can to extract sharply distinct reactions to his questions and comments," occasionally siding with one the guests. (Bahry 2001: 104) Ironically, by siding with a particular guest (giving "priority to commercial or political considerations over professional ones" and impeding "fairness," "balance" and "credibility") such an approach seems a complete violation of the first article of Al-Jazeera's code of ethics (see Document 1. Al-Jazeera Code of Ethics).

Since the early 1990s, the Arab mediascape has undergone profound changes, exemplified by increasing competition, professionalization, and in some cases, a departure from government control. CNN's exclusive coverage of the first Gulf War prompted development of transnational broadcast media in the Arab world as an alternative to the otherwise predominant American framing of events. (Gaballah 2005; Miles 2005; El-Nawawy and Iskandar 2002; Sakr 2001) Decades of government control over the media had previously instigated a climate of distrust amongst the public. A memorable example concerns a false broadcast by Gamal Abdel Nasser's *Sawt al-Arab* radio during the 1967 Arab-Israeli war. The station's declaration that Arab armies had triumphed over their Israeli foes was repeated in local media until foreign sources revealed that the Arab armies had in fact suffered a humiliating defeat. Similarly, the Saudi media failed to report for two full days Iraq's 1990 invasion of Kuwait. "All the media came to be regarded, quite rightly, as appendages of the government, which only ever echoed, never investigated or criticized, what their leaders said." (Miles 2005: 25) After the failed BBC Arabic television channel, many considered Al-Jazeera a revolution in the Arab media. (Gaballah 2005) London Bureau Chief Mostefa Souag explains that "Al-Jazeera was the first time Arabs discovered it was possible to have an Arab institution that they could respect." (in Miles 2005: 34)

On the political dimension, satellite broadcasting's liberating potential in the Arab world has garnered much speculation as an *Economist* special report illustrates:

> "It is one thing to learn of different, perhaps attractive, lifestyles in foreign cultures by way of Hollywood movies; it is quite another to see them being practiced next door. Even the most purdahed of Saudi women are liable to observe that driving cars, forbidden to them, is quite normal for their sisters not only in distant, decadent America, but also in nearby Kuwait or Dubai. Syrians or Egyptians can see that real elections take place not just in rich Christian Europe, but in neighboring Palestine and Iraq. Such innovations are no longer perhaps just for people 'like them,' but for people 'like us.'" (Economist 2005)

These arguments, however, may be placed in a much older debate concerning the democratization capacity of the media. (Mill 1869; Siebert *et al.* 1956; Keane 1991; O'Neill 1998; Hiebert and Gibbons 2000) Traditional liberal media theory dominates this discussion. (Siebert *et al.* 1956) The liberal model presents a normative view inasmuch as it assumes that media systems reflect the system of those societies in which they evolve. Alternative models attempting to defy the euro-centricity of their predecessors have also been suggested. (Curran and Park 2000: 13) Carey highlights a typical argument for democratic development when suggesting that "mass communication and media enhance and protect the practice of democracy in democratic states, and agitate the masses for demanding a gradual implementation of democracy." (Carey 1993: 2) If Al-Jazeera truly operates independently, the test of time will determine its role in the Arab world's democratic development. However, one cannot assume that free speech on the airwaves will necessarily lead to democracy in the Middle East. (Alterman 1999)

Al-Jazeera's motto, constantly advertised on the channel, has been a source of relentless criticism and support. (Al-Zaidi 2003) Yet the dilemma posited by a news channel providing "the opinion and the other opinion" as its main editorial line seems contradictory when placed in the wider context of news reporting. On a theoretical plane, news reporting in itself consists in stating facts as they are presented in news reports. Media theory has nevertheless established the significance of "the agenda-setting function of the mass media." (McCombs and Shaw 1972) In contrast, the motto may easily be applied to talks shows, a forum for news analysis and socio-political discourse. While Al-Jazeera may have first succeeded in providing a source of news alternative to Western sources and Arabic official or governmental sources, its editorial line has at times impeded its credibility. The channel therefore toes a very fine line between credibility and integrity. By airing different and opposing viewpoints, Al-Jazeera arguably externalized the complexity of the Arab World through the eyes of both Arab and non-Arab representatives. Such an approach may deliver a seemingly democratic freedom of expression, exhilarating for numerous citizens of those Arab nations devoid of a democratic process, but no more than a mere illusion. The channel has thus made itself both hero and victim. By replicating the same conversations that take place on the streets and in the living rooms of Damascus, Beirut, Cairo and elsewhere—namely illustrated by the lack of references and credible sources deployed by the hosts and guests on the channel's talk shows—Al-Jazeera demonstrates the varying complexities of Arab societies toward internal and external criticism. But the channel stops short of acting upon these varying voices.

In contrast, Senior Correspondent Mostefa Souag warns that Al-Jazeera is not the voice of the Arab world, but rather has become a trusted news source because it offers a balanced view. "It's important to show the views that are there without judging them," he adds. However, if the channel truly reflects these wide-ranging views, one must consider how the views are presented or framed. Within the post-national context posited by such technology as satellite television, it is necessary to re-evaluate the communication process and consider the saliency of other actors at hand. While facilitating the entire communication process, globalization also transmits perceptions, values and belief systems. On a global scale, the mass media serve as the encoder of the information source, providing varying interpretation of the original data. As Al-Jazeera Ramallah bureau chief Walid al-Omary explains, "We try to keep balance in our coverage and just try to give the people the facts and let them judge what is happening, but it is not easy at all—not easy at all for us—and I am living in this society [...] At the same time, Al-Jazeera is not the UN and it faces and sufferers the same dangers as the people." (in Miles 2005: 78) In this sense, Al-Jazeera necessarily reflects Arab opinions through its provision of a public space for dialogue. Globalization requires reviewing and adapting to notions in contemporary reality comprising "what we call culture, mutations of national sentiment, relationships between state and society, perceptions of the Other, stereotypes, representations, the opening of other societies and religions, the Western model's crisis, tacit qualms toward globalization, change in the types of national identities, the impact of mass media..." (Wolton 2003: 35) Senders and receivers interpret the meaning of a particular message and naturally infuse the communication process with their own cosmology, which explains the plurality of responses generated by the channel's coverage.

Conclusion

When it first came into being, Al-Jazeera stood as an oddity in the Arab world, rife with control of the press and ministries of information. Al-Jazeera's relative freedom owes much to the series of political, social and economic reforms enacted by the Emir of Qatar. These reforms both expanded the news audience and enabled increased competition for better journalists. Bahry explains that "until the advent of Al-Jazeera, Arabs did not pay much attention to the media in their own countries. They considered this information as little more than an extension of the views of their own governments, echoing official speeches and reporting on the activities of leaders." (2001: 90) The news channel defends its status as the Arab world's first television station to criticize Arab governments and regimes where such criticism was long considered a taboo, allegedly favoring dialogue over rejection, criticism over dismissal. In attempting to present the opinion *and* the other opinion, the channel invariably lends more focus to "the other opinion," that which is usually undermined. As a consequence, a division between "us"—Arabs and/or Muslims—and "them"—the "West"—constantly emerges. Al-Jazeera's motto has brought both success and failure to the channel as it stresses integration and differentiation on an equal plane. Rather than observe coherence, the viewer watches cacophony, an orchestra without a conductor. In order to achieve better harmony, the channel requires a "conductor" or conductors to tune the different voices, to offer a more holistic understanding of contrasting viewpoints on current events. Yet as a news media, Al-Jazeera must limit description or adoption of such a role to the semantic level. The new challenge for the 21st century may then lie in how to create harmony out of the wide range of differing voices by not alienating them but rather providing a tune to which they may all contribute.

A framing analysis applied to the January and March 2005 episodes of 3 Al-Jazeera programs—*Lil-Nissa' Faqat, Al-Ittijah al-Muakiss* and *Hiwar Maftouh*—revealed a tendency in the selected program to present issues in a dichotomous manner, often caught between an imagined "West" and "Arab world." Speakers also regularly evoked the West, and particularly the United States as a reference point and source of data while their very own discourse and the choice of topics seemed atypical of broader Arab concerns. The different hosts interjected a number of times in order to channel the discussion in particular ways and at times presented dubious suppositions as facts. The episodes' discourse most often depicts a world in black and white, with little attention to the subtle differences underlying the discussion. As talk shows, these programs feature different tenants of an issue aired live—neither edited nor censored—the overall discourse therefore presents strong tendencies toward particular biases. The media, and in this case, Al-Jazeera, may play the role of messenger, but not that of a perfect messenger. The messages carried have already experienced the numerous encoding and decoding processes posited in a basic model of communications. (Shannon and Weaver 1963) As a means of translation and transformation of meaning across time and space, hosts, guests, callers, but also program producers and editors, play both consciously and unconsciously on all the subtleties, confusions and misunderstandings of Arab societies. In light of the consensus emerging on the framing of particular, guests, host, callers and viewers alike often come to recognize certain viewpoints as self-evident. The channel presents the current status, enforces it, and criticizes it. While providing an illusion of democracy on the airwaves, Al-Jazeera does not, however, provide for significant actual change. This trend is not particular to Al-Jazeera alone. Rather, as Future Television (Lebanon) talk-show host Zaven Kouyoumjian posits, "media people in the Middle East are more advanced than the society itself." Furthermore, "globalization means that on Arab TV you'll find the same décor, the same plastic surgery and the same formats as in the West. But it's artificial, and doesn't mirror the social evolution of society." (Kouyoumjian in Power and Haddad 2005: 54)

While certain patterns were detected throughout the various January and March 2005 episodes, a generalization of these trends to the channel as a whole requires further research. Future work may choose to analyze several programs, at least two or three, over a longer period of time. It is also recommended to include research relevant to the specific topics raised in the episodes analyzed below. Matching the detected forms of discourse with events concurrent with the time of the episode may especially provide useful insight due to the saliency of contexts. An impulse model, also suggested for future research, involves a structured interview with the policy-maker, here Al-Jazeera's producers, editors, spokesperson and other representatives. In order to provide an appropriate background to the discussion, attention should be given to the Qatari government's role and reasoning for creating and maintaining the channel. The 1990 information revolution in the Arab world and current Arab mediascape should also be assessed further for additional context.

As concerns the broader analysis presented throughout this paper, further research could provide a content analysis of the channel's actual coverage, as featured in its news bulletins and live reports. Quantitative data may be gathered by deploying a policy-media interaction model. A traditional method consists in erecting categories (e.g. empathy vs. distance) and subsequently counting the number of words relative to each category. Such research would enable an evaluation of the channel in relation to the CNN effect or the "manufacturing consent" thesis. (Robinson 2002) While the former indicates media's ability to instigate policy change, the latter refers to media replicating government positions. This method was not chosen for this work, as the categorization and allocation of words was deemed normative.

In breaching taboos and uncovering sensitive issues, Al-Jazeera has allowed previously forbidden discourse to emerge from behind closed doors into the public field, especially as concerns the Arab world. The contrasting responses the channel has generated indicate that it provides merely a reflection of the reality it seeks to portray. Al-Jazeera may then resemble a messenger with less stringent filters than government-controlled media. Nevertheless, such an editorial policy implies that Al-Jazeera toes a very fine line subject as concerns pressure from governments and other interested parties. In so doing, the channel's framing of events is not linear, but rather depends upon the divergent opinions voiced in response to particular issues. At the same time, Al-Jazeera's seeming refusal to take sides may mark both its success and its demise in a climate rife with opposing viewpoints. However, if, as claimed by Al-Jazeera staff and supporters, the channel does represent the first "free" media of the Arab world, then one should not be surprised that this same freedom is misused and abused. Therein lies the channel's controversy. As Mohammadi suggests, "The only way culture can grow is to open itself to other cultures, to interact critically and freely." (Mohammadi 1998: 271)

Olivia Qusaibaty

Appendix

Document 1. Al-Jazeera Code of Ethics
(Al-Jazeera 2004)

Being a globally oriented media service, Al-jazeera shall determinedly adopt the following code of ethics in pursuance of the vision and mission it has set for itself:

1. Adhere to the journalistic values of honesty, courage, fairness, balance, independence, credibility and diversity, giving no priority to commercial or political considerations over professional ones.

2. Endeavor to get to the truth and declare it in our dispatches, programs and news bulletins unequivocally in a manner which leaves no doubt about its validity and accuracy.

3. Treat our audiences with due respect and address every issue or story with due attention to present a clear, factual and accurate picture while giving full consideration to the feelings of victims of crime, war, persecution and disaster, their relatives and our viewers, and to individual privacy and public decorum.

4. Welcome fair and honest media competition without allowing it to affect adversely our standards of performance so that getting a "scoop" will not become an end in itself.

5. Present diverse points of view and opinions without bias or partiality.

6. Recognize diversity in human societies with all their races, cultures and beliefs and their values and intrinsic individualities in order to present unbiased and faithful reflection of them.

7. Acknowledge a mistake when it occurs, promptly correct it and ensure it does not recur.

8. Observe transparency in dealing with news and news sources while adhering to internationally established practices concerning the rights of these sources.

9. Distinguish between news material, opinion and analysis to avoid the pitfalls of speculation and propaganda.

10. Stand by colleagues in the profession and offer them support when required, particularly in light of the acts of aggression and harassment to which journalists are subjected at times. Cooperate with Arab and international journalistic unions and associations to defend freedom of the press.

Table 1. 2000-2004 total adult literacy rates (aged 15 and above)
(UIS 2004)

Country	Total (%)	Male (%)	Female (%)
Algeria**	68.9	78	59.6
Bahrain**	88.5	91.5	84.2
Comoros**	56.2	63.5	49.1
Egypt*	55.6	67.2	43.6
Israel**	95.3	97.3	93.4
Jordan**	90.9	95.5	85.9
Kuwait**	82.9	84.7	81
Libya**	81.7	91.8	70.7
Mauritania**	41.2	51.5	31.3
Morocco**	50.7	63.3	38.3
Oman**	74.4	82	65.4
Qatar*	84.2	84.9	82.3
Saudi Arabia**	77.9	84.1	69.5
Sudan**	59.9	70.8	49.1
Syria*	82.9	91	74.2
Tunisia**	73.2	83.1	63.1
UAE**	77.3	75.6	80.7
Yemen**	49	69.5	28.5

*Self-declaration
**UIS estimates
Figures for Djibouti, Iraq, the Palestinian Authority and Lebanon were not available.

Table 2. Arab Media Preferences
(Telhami 2005)*

Primary Station	Jordan	Morocco	Lebanon	Saudi Arabia	UAE	Egypt
Al-Jazeera	62%	54%	44%	44%	46%	66%
Al-Arabiya	7%	8%	7%	9%	19%	5%
2M	NA	11%	NA	NA	NA	NA
LBC	4%	NA	29%	2%	1%	NA
Abu Dhabi TV	3%	1%	1%	22%	17%	NA

Olivia Qusaibaty

Secondary Station	Jordan	Morocco	Lebanon	Saudi Arabia	UAE	Egypt
Al-Jazeera	14%	17%	25%	23%	21%	12%
Al-Arabiya	39%	32%	26%	28%	30%	28%

*Conducted in May 2004, this Zogby International and University of Maryland poll consisted of 3,300 male and female adult Arab viewers in urban regions of 6 nations: Morocco, Egypt, Jordan, Lebanon, Saudi Arabia, and the United Arab Emirates. The above responses were provided to the following research question: "When you watch international news, which of the following network's news broadcasts do you watch most often? And which network's news broadcast is your second choice?"

Table 3. Sources of Attitudes Toward the US
(Telhami 2005)*

	Jordan	Morocco	Lebanon	Saudi Arabia	UAE	Egypt
American Values	16%	18%	9%	10%	9%	<1%
American Policy	76%	79%	80%	86%	75%	90%
Not Sure	7%	3%	11%	6%	16%	<1%

*This survey was conducted in the same conditions as above, but with the following research question: "Would you say that your attitudes toward the United States are based more on American values or on American policy in the Middle East?"

Table 4. Main Live and Recorded Al-Jazeera Programs
(Al-Jazeera 2003-2005)[3]

Program name	Host	Description
MAIN WEEKLY LIVE PROGRAMS		
Akthar min Ra'i (More than One Opinion)	Sami Haddad	Three guests debate the issue of the week deemed most newsworthy. Broadcast from London.
Al-Ittijah al-Mua'kiss (The Opposite Direction)	Faisal al-Qasim	Debate between two guests taking opposite

---

[3] The programs listed here were broadcast regularly between December 2004 and August 2005 (the main period of observation for this research). Al-Jazeera introduced a new format as well as new programs in June 2005. Certain programs have had different hosts in the past than those listed here.

		views on an issue
Ash-Shari'ah wal-Haya (Islamic law and life)	Khadija bin Qana	Discussion on contemporary issues from an Islamic perspective. Often features Sheikh Yousef al-Qardawy
Bila Hudud (Without Bounds)	Ahmed Mansour	Interview of a prominent figure where the host adopts a position critical of the guest
Hiwar Maftouh (Open Dialogue)	Ghassan bin Jeddo	Discussion with several guests (usually three or more) and often a live audience
Lil-Nissa' Faqat (For Women Only)	Louna ash-Shebl	Debate with 3 or more guests on contemporary women's issues. Discontinued in June 2005.
Min Washington (From Washington)	Hafez al-Mirazi	Discussion with 2 or more guests on issues pertaining to the US or US-Arab relations
OTHER LIVE PROGRAMS		
Al-Malif al-Usbu'i (The Weekly File)	Jameel Azr	Review of the main news stories of the week
Ma Wara' al-Khabar (What's Behind the News)	Various rotating (including Jomana Namour, Mohammed Kreeshan, Faisal al-Qasim)	30-minute discussion with several out-of-studio guests on a news topic of the day. Broadcast daily since June 2005.
Minbar al-Jazeera (Al-Jazeera's Platform)	Various (including Hassan Jamoul, Abd as-Samd Nasser, Leila ash-Shaib)	Invites viewers to comment on a chosen topic via phone, mail, email, or facsimile
MAIN RECORDED PROGRAMS		
Al-Kitab Khair Jaliss (The Book is a good companion)	Khaled al-Horoub	Discusses a book (literature or socio-political commentary) with the author(s) and

	critics	
Arshifihim wa Tarikhna (Their Archives and our History)	None	Overview of main Arab historical figures and events
Doroub (Paths)	None	Weekly interviews with prominent cultural figures and students
Liqa' al-Yawm (Today's meeting)	Various	Interviews with prominent political figures in the news
Ma'a Heikal (With Heikal)	Mohammed Hassanin Heikal	Historical overview presented by Mohammed Hassanin Heikal
Murasilu al-Jazeera (Al-Jazeera Correspondents)	Mohammed al-Bourini	Socio-cultural stories from Al-Jazeera's correspondents around the world (weekly)
Nuqta Sakhina (Hot Spot)	Ass'ad Taha	Documentary series examining "hot spots" around the world
Shahid 'ala al-Asr (Eyewitness to the Century)	Ahmed Mansour	Recorded interview with prominent historical figures of the past. Each guest is often interviewed for several episodes. Discontinued in June 2005.
Taht al-Majhar (Under Scrutiny)	Various	Investigates socio-political issues
Zina (Fashion)	Rosie	Highlights trends in fashion in Europe, the Arab world and elsewhere
Ziyara Khassa (Special Visit)	Sami Kulaib	Interviews with prominent figures in their homes around the world

Table 5. Selection of Al-Jazeera Programs for Framing Analysis
(Lil-Nissa' Faqat 2005; Al-Ittijah al-Muakiss 2005; Hiwar Maftouh 2005)

Lil-Nissa' Faqat

DATE	3-Jan-05	11-Jan-05	17-Jan-05
HOST	Fairuz Zayani	Fairuz Zayani	Louna ash-Shebl
TOPIC	Future diseases for the Tsunami survivors	Discovering girls' secrets	The sexual exploitation of children
GUESTS	Amany Haroun (psychology professor at Ain Shams university); Anissa Amyn Mar'y (psychologist), Fatima Nozrath (welfare assistant at the Sri Lankan Islamic Center	Mozaha al-Maliky (Psychologist and professor in Qatar), Mouna Younis (Manager of the English section for the liberation of family and youth in Islam)	Sarour Qarwany (Consultant for humanitarian development possibilities), Maha al-Hamssa (Manager of the program for children's protection in the Jordan office of UNICEF), Iza Karim (Professor of meeting education in the national centre for social and criminal research)
MAIN ISSUES	Effects of the Tsunami disaster in Sumatra, extensive accidents of the disaster on the survivors, rise of a cure for shocks from the disasters, the size of the disaster in Sri Lanka, the entrusted role by nations for scientists to resolve the disaster issues.	Effects of globalisation on the youth's behaviour, the interests and engagements of the Arab girl, the impact of the Internet on girls, the family circle in childhood and informing the generations, the possible roles an Arab girl can play, the feeling of despotic emptiness in our girls.	Examples of children's sexual exploitation in Morocco, the sexual exploitation of children and the lack of statistics, the mental effect of assaults on children, the social effect of children's sexual exploitation, ways to identify molested children, protective methods against sexual harassment.

Olivia Qusaibaty

DATE	24-Jan-05	31-Jan-05	7-Mar-05
HOST	Louna ash-Shebl	Louna ash-Shebl	Louna ash-Shebl
TOPIC	The culture of voluntary work in women's charitable organisations	Sexual education for children	The New York conference and women's rights
GUESTS	Amany Qandyl (Executive Director of the Arab network for national/ domestic organisation), Iqabal Doghan (former President of the Lebanese Women's council), Mana Shishtar (activist in volunteer work domain for many charitable organisations)	Muzain Assyran Huballah (specialist in clinical and analytical psychology), Huba Qatab (specialist of sexual medicine and marital relations), Adiya abu Ghraib (Professor of methodology in the national centre for educational research), Abila Mohammed al-Kahalawy (Al-Azhar al-Sharif University Professor)	Azat al-Hur Marwa (General coordinator for the Lebanese national project to eliminate discrimination against women), Moha Aby Diya Shimass (Head of the Woman's Centre for the direction of constitution in Cairo), Aliya al-Karady (Iraqi researcher for Gender and Women's affairs)

MAIN ISSUES	The role of the Arab woman in the affected areas, evaluation of the performance of Arab charitable organisations, Reasons for the slow reaction to disasters, women's role in the work of charitable organisations, customs and traditions controlling women's work as volunteers, the politicisation of the Tsunami disaster	The questions of children and adult's shyness, bodily contact and its affect on children, the necessity to grant children answers to embarrassing questions, the mother and father's responsibility and the role of curricula, the relations between puberty and legal age for religious rituals, the exemplary method for dealing with adolescent girls and boys	History of the conferences for women from Mexico to New York, ignoring cultural differences in the Beijing agreement, civil society organisations and the external agendas, true sexual freedom and the woman's enablement.

DATE	14-Mar-05	28-Mar-05
HOST	Louna ash-Shebl	Louna ash-Shebl
TOPIC	The Kuwaiti woman's voting and candidacy rights	The difficulties of Western Muslim women
GUESTS	Ma'asoma al-Mobarek (professor of international relations, Kuwait University), Khola al-'Atika (activist in the domain of women's rights), Walid al-Tobtana (Member of the national Kuwaiti council)	Batol Al Nawma (Head of educational research in the Islamic organisation of London), Lina Lorenz coordinator of the Oslo network for freedom of tenets and debts), Iman Ramaddan (Member of the Muslim women group in

		London), Bylar Saad (professor of flag meetings in the Florida Academy)
MAIN ISSUES	Women's candidacy rights and the idea of general (genderless) leadership, the woman's candidacy between Islamic law and politics, the woman between political and social work, political reform and its impact on the role of women, the woman's candidacy and the effect of the different Kuwaiti (religious) factions, questions and comments from the viewers, the social map of Kuwait and women's participation, the woman and true international pressure on the Kuwaiti society.	The status of Western Muslim women in London, Reasons for western women's embracement of Islam, The conversion from Christianity to Islam, Reasons for an increased embracement of Western women Islam, intentionally incorrect translations of the Qur'an, Problems of the Muslim woman in America

Al-Ittijah al-Muakiss

DATE	4-Jan-05	11-Jan-05	18-Jan-05
HOST	Faisal al-Qasim	Faisal al-Qasim	Faisal al-Qasim
TOPIC	The human development reports	The Iraqi elections	The [Nairobi] Peace Accord in Sudan
GUESTS	Manir Shafiq (author of *Humanitarian Development or Globalisation: A Critical Study of the U.N. Arab Human Development Reports 2002-2003*) and Nader Fayad (Egyptian writer and researcher)	Nouri al-Mouradi (Official spokesman of the communist party) and Khalaf Abd as-Samd (Secretary General for the organization of the Iraqi martyr)	Ghazy Suleiman (Chairman of the National Coalition to Restore Democracy in Sudan) and Hassan Saty (Sudanese journalist and writer)

MAIN ISSUES	Development reports: between truth and deceit; development reports and the Arab nations; the effect of the new world order on Arab development; the reports: between objectivity and methodological mistakes; responsibility of the new imperialism on the Arabs' backwardness.	Reasons for the uproar regarding the elections, [Ali] al-Sistani's position on the elections and Jihad (holy war fighting0, examples of elections under occupation, electoral law and method to count the voices, opposition parties and the elections, the elections in light of the designated government's presence.	Evaluation of the peace accord, religious, cultural, and political pluralism and the danger of dividing Sudan. Participation of the spectators, diving the wealth between the North and the South and its problems, the foreign role behind the peace accord and its implications, the situation of Sudan during the transitional period.

DATE	25-Jan-05	1-Mar-05	8-Mar-05
HOST	Faisal al-Qasim	Faisal al-Qasim	Faisal al-Qasim
TOPIC	Spain and the Arab community	Police states and friction in Lebanon and Syria	Popular resistance movements
GUESTS	Yahya abu Zakriya (Algerian researcher and journalist, author of the book Islam and the West), Ignacio Gutiérrez de Terán (Professor of the Autónoma University in Madrid and head of the liberal magazine al-Watan al-Araby)	Abd al-Razaq Eid (Founding member of the committee for reviving civil society in Syria) and Karim al-Shybany (Head of the Syrian National Democratic Party)	Ahmad al-Najdawi (Ba'ath party leader) and Mohammed al-Mousawi (Iraqi writer and politician)

Olivia Qusaibaty

MAIN ISSUES	Date and nature of the relation between Spain and the Arabs, Hispano-Arab relations lecture, mentions of detentions and judgements during the Franco era, Racism of Spanish politics against the Arabs, Range of previous detentions of Arabs in Spain.	The Syrian question – between conspiracy and reduction; the Syrian internal movement versus the security core, the justifications to target Syria and the levels of escalation, the discourse of the opposition against Syria, the reasons behind the Syrian political rigidity	The Intifada of one million in Lebanon, the external intervention in Arab demonstrations, similarity between Lebanon and Venezuela, American's varying respect for the people's desires, the Lebanese Intifada and accusations that it was directed by America.

DATE	15-Mar-05	22-Mar-05	29-Mar-05
HOST	Faisal al-Qasim	Faisal al-Qasim	Faisal al-Qasim
TOPIC	The relation between terrorism and colonisation in the Arab world	Hezbollah	The American invasion of Iraq and its favoured reforms
GUESTS	Mohamed al-Bodeiry (Liberal Egyptian writer) and Kamal Shatyla (Head of the Lebanese Popular Council)	'Issam Abu Jumra (Deputy head of the transitional military government in the auxiliary government) and Mi'an Bashour (Secretary General for the Arab conference)	Faryd al-Ghadry (Head of the opposition Syrian reform party and founder of the Syrian democratic alliance) and George Hajjar (professor of political science and international relations)

| MAIN ISSUES | The return of colonization and its reasons, historic review of colonization, internal problems and external interventions, Arab terrorism and the American scenario, the American "Trojan horse" and the Zionist program, spectators' interventions, Holako or Al-Mostassam Billah | Hezbollah's popular standing, the situation with weapons and the Palestinian resistance, Hezbollah and the Israeli opposition threat, external support for the Lebanese opposition, the international situation for Hezbollah's legitimacy, situation of the Lebanese army before the assembly, opposition against Hezbollah. | The American intervention, between necessity and lie, American impact of the occupation in Iraq, Reversals of the Iraqi occupation on the Arabic scene. |

Hiwar Maftouh

DATE	1-Jan-05	8-Jan-05	15-Jan-05
HOST	Ghassan bin Jeddo	Ghassan bin Jeddo	Ghassan bin Jeddo
TOPIC	The Arab future and the issue of reform	The Palestinian electoral scene	Political Tension in Lebanon
GUESTS	Burhan Ghalioun (Professor of sociology at the University Paris 3 and Director of the Centre for Contemporary Oriental Studies) and Moustafa al-Faqi (Head of the Egyptian National Assembly's	Khaled Arif (senior Fatah official in Lebanon), Suheil al-Natour (Palestinian affairs analyst and council member of the Democratic Front for the Liberation of Palestine), Marwan abdel Aal (representative of	Michel Aoun (Leader of the Free Patriotic Movement residing in exile) and Ali Hassan al-Khalil (former minister and current deputy in Parliament).

	Foreign Affairs Committee).	the Popular Front for the Liberation of Palestine in Lebanon), Yasser al-Zaatara (Palestinian Islamic writer).	
MAIN ISSUES	The truth about the Arab status at the current stage; reasons for the silence of the Arab audiences; Arabs: between reform and change; reform: between civil society and authority; the internal dispute about openness and external intervention.	The electoral strategies of the Democratic Front; the role of the Popular Front in the general elections; criticisms directed toward Abu Mazin [Mahmoud Abbas] and the Fatah movement; the Palestinian national constants toward Abu Mazin; criticism directed toward Mostafa al-Bargouti; projected national criticism of the Fatah movement.	Michel Aoun, exile and the relation with Syria; the Amal [Future] Movement, its position with respect to Aoun and his return; Aoun's position on the Taif Agreement [the Document of National Accord], the [Lebanese] constitution, and Israel; the position of the Lebanese forces and the incarceration of Samir Jaja; Aoun and his opinion on the elections.

DATE	22-Jan-05	5-Mar-05	12-Mar-05
HOST	Ghassan bin Jeddo	Ghassan bin Jeddo	Ghassan bin Jeddo
TOPIC	The Iraqi position after the elections	Lebanon after the government's resignation and al-Assad's speech	The anticipated presidential elections in Iran

GUESTS	Abdel-Amir al-Rikaby (Secretary of the preparatory conference for the Iraqi Council of Establishment); Abu Maysim al-Juwahiry (representative of the Islamic Da'wah [Call] Party in Iraq); Mathny Harth al-Dary (spokesman on behalf of the Muslim Ulama Committee)	Wyam Wahab (resigned Minister of the Environment); Ahmed Fatfat (Deputy of the opposition); Nassib Hatait (Secretary of the committee of followers of the meeting of Ain al-Tina); Elias Atollah (Secretary of the Democratic Left movement); Amin al-Jamil (Former Lebanese president).	Ali Akbar Walaity (Top guiding Adviser for international relations and candidate for the presidency of the Iranian republic); Bashir Nafa'a (Historian and follower of Iranian affairs); Mohamed al-Said Sa'id (Deputy Manager of the Al-Ahram Center for Strategic Studies); Taher 'Adwan (President and Chief Editor of the Jordanian newspaper al-Arab al-Yawm)
MAIN ISSUES	The elections' opposite reasons; the American intervention and the legitimacy of the elections; the situation of the Iraqi community in Iran; a corroborative majority that refuses the minority for the elections; criticism directed against the American ambassador, John Negroponte; reasons for the Muslim Ulama Committee's withdrawal from the elections.	Reasons for the government's resignation and the role of the opposition; the Lebanese street: between support and opposition; the opposition and its situation from Assad's speech and from the resistance; the investigation into the assassination of Hariri; Arabism in Lebanon and the possibility of a relation with Israel; the American role in the events in Lebanon.	The party responsible for violence and terrorism; the Muslim Brotherhood: between strictness and moderation; the difference between resistance and terrorism; the Islamic group in Lebanon and the extent of its sway to violence; speech of the Islamic group; reasons for the appearance of violence in the Gulf states.

Olivia Qusaibaty

DATE	19-Mar-05	26-Mar-05
HOST	Ghassan bin Jeddo	Ghassan bin Jeddo
TOPIC	The Arab popular movement	Dialogue of the Islamic Forces Group with Washington
GUESTS	'Issam Khalifa (Professor of History in the Lebanese University) Assa'ad Abu Khalil (Professor of political humanities at the California University); Abu al-'Ala Maddy (from the foundation of the middle party and the Kiffayah movement)	Alistair Cook (Manager of the International Conflict Resolution Centre) Nowaf al-Mousawi (Head of Hizbullah International Relations and member of the CIA political office) 'Ezam al-Tamamy (Manager of the Institute of Islamic Political Thought in London)
MAIN ISSUES	popular pressure and opportunities for change; popular pressure and the external branches, associated interjections; national democracy: between the agenda and the foreign agenda; Arab popular movements in the context of global movements; Lebanon as an example of the frustration of the Arab people.	Sense and goal of the Beirut meeting; Important range of the dialogue with the Americans; The Americans and the dialogue with Hamas and Hizbullah; points of the Beirtu talk; possibility of raising Hamas and Hizbullah out of terrorism.

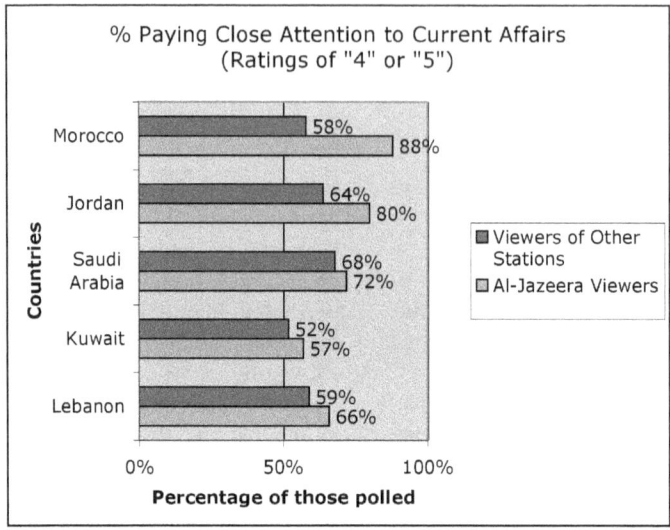

Figure 1. Television Viewers' Attention to Current Affairs
(Saad 2002)

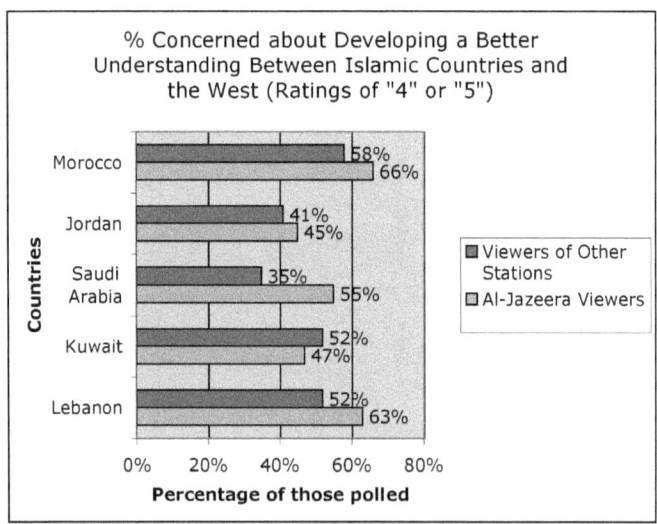

Figure 2. Television Viewers' Concerns toward Improving Relations between Western and Islamic Cultures
(Saad 2002)

Olivia Qusaibaty

Bibliography

Abdallah, Maher. 11 August 2004. "A fear of free speech."
London: The Guardian.

Abu-Lughod, Lila. 1993. "Finding a place for Islam: Egyptian
television serials and the national interest." Chicago:
Public Culture. 5.3: 494-513.

Abu Odeh, Adnan. 25 May 2004. "Thanks to Abu Ghraib, Al-
Jazeera has Gained Breathing Space" Beirut: *The Daily
Star*.
<www.dailystar.com.lb/article.asp?edition_ID=10&arti
cle_ID=4324&categ_id=5>

Agence France-Presse (AFP). 31 January 2005. "L'État du
Qatar désireux de privatiser Al-Jazira" Doha: Agence France
Presse.

13 July 2004. "Arab Media under Spotlight at Qatar
Forum" Beirut: *The Daily Star*.
<www.dailystar.com.lb/article.asp?edition_ID=10&articl
e_ID=6174&categ_id=2>

Ajami, Fouad. 18 November 2001. "What the Muslim World is
Watching." *New York Times Magazine*. Late ed. 48.

Al-Alami, Mohammad. 8 January 2005. Washington: personal
interview by the author with Al-Jazeera's Washington
bureau Chief Correspondent.

Al-Basri, Daoud. 13 April 2005. "Qatar…Wa Qanat al-
Jazeera…Marara (biny Mara)?" [Qatar…and the Al-
Jazeera Channel…Bitterness (Bitter Times)?] *Elaph.*
<www.elaph.com/elaphweb/ElaphWriter/2005/4/55053
.htm>

Al-Ghamdy, Qeinan. 3 April 2005. "'Al-Jazeera' min Qatar,
wa Isqat al-Janssia: Kam Baqy fyl-Doha ba'd
Rahilihim" [Al-Jazeera from Qatar and revoking
citizenship: How many left in Doha after they remove
them?]. Riyadh, Saudi Arabia: Al-Watan.
<www.alwatan.com.sa/daily/2005-04-
03/writers/writers07.htm>

Al-Ittijah al-Muakiss. [The Opposite Direction]. 29 March
2005. "Al-ghozo al-Amriky al-Iraq wa 'Atharahu 3ala
al-Isslahat." [The American invasion of Iraq and its
favoured reforms]. Hosted by Faisal al-Qasim. Doha:
Al-Jazeera satellite channel.
<www.aljazeera.net/NR/exeres/CD9E3C33-E38C-
4F45-A7B4-8884716F94CA.htm>
22 March 2005. "Hezbollah." Hosted by Faisal al-
Qasim. Doha: Al-Jazeera satellite channel.
<www.aljazeera.net/NR/exeres/7190A1F8-1D5C-
4A61-9C7D-F99FB6E08492.htm>
15 March 2005. "Al-Alaqa bayna al-Istibdad wal-
ista'amar fyl-'alim al-'araby." [The relation between
terrorism and colonisation in the Arab world]. Hosted
by Faisal al-Qasim. Doha: Al-Jazeera satellite channel.
<www.aljazeera.net/NR/exeres/1CA8F39F-BE73-
4EDB-B82B-348057976943>
8 March 2005. "Intifaddat Sha'abia." [Popular
Resistance Movements]. Hosted by Faisal al-Qasim.
Doha: Al-Jazeera satellite channel.
<www.aljazeera.net/NR/exeres/E64EF771-DBAD-
4A9E-83A9-4996A122731B.htm>
1 March 2005. "Al-siyasa al-amniya wal-hitqan fy
Lubnan wa Soriya." [Police states and friction in
Lebanon and Syria]. Hosted by Faisal al-Qasim. Doha:
Al-Jazeera satellite channel.
<www.aljazeera.net/NR/exeres/8DC9FD37-448A-
443E-929D-B79B4536F901.htm>
25 January 2005. "Isbaniya wal-Jaliyat al-Arabiya."
[Spain and the Arab community]. Hosted by Faisal al-
Qasim. Doha: Al-Jazeera satellite channel.
<www.aljazeera.net/NR/exeres/4DA0ECA6-D4CD-
4F9D-A9F1-ABBCD2AA24DB.htm>
18 January 2005. "Itifaq as-Salam fyl-Sudan." [The
[Nairobi] Peace Accord in Sudan]. Hosted by Faisal al-
Qasim. Doha: Al-Jazeera satellite channel.

<www.aljazeera.net/NR/exeres/95F0AEB3-CA44-
4695-98CE-AA43CDE9B528.htm>
11 January 2005. "Al-Intikhabat al-Iraqiya." [The Iraqi
elections]. Hosted by Faisal al-Qasim. Doha: Al-Jazeera
satellite channel.
<www.aljazeera.net/NR/exeres/91B3C6EB-E8FD-
481A-82AA-4EB79A15FCCC.htm>
4 January 2005. "Al-Taqarir al-tanmiya al-bashriya."
[The [U.N.] Human Development Reports]. Hosted by
Faisal al-Qasim. Doha: Al-Jazeera satellite channel.
<www.aljazeera.net/NR/exeres/58081993-E197-4C5C-
99CF-F2C4D3C9AEED.htm>

Al-Jazeera. Consulted January 2003 – August 2005. "Al-
Jazeera.net." Doha, Qatar: <www.al-jazeera.net>

Al-Jazeera. 15 July 2004. "Aljazeera Code of Ethics" Doha:
Al-Jazeera. First announced 12 July, 2004 at Doha
Conference.
<http://english.aljazeera.net/NR/exeres/07256105-
B2FC-439A-B255-D830BB238EA1.htm>

Al-Jazeera English. Consulted January 2004 – August 2005.
Al-Jazeera.net English. Doha, Qatar:
<www.english.aljazeera.net>

Al-Kasim, Faisal. 2005. "The Opposite Direction: A Program
which Changed the Face of Arab Television" in Zayani,
Mohamed. *The Al-Jazeera Phenomenon: Critical
Perspectives on New Arab Media*. Paradigm Publishers.
93-106.

Al-Shammari, Sulaiman Jazia. 1999. *Al-Buad al-Qawmi fyl-
Qanat al-Jazeera* [The National Dimension in the Al-
Jazeera Channel]. Doha: Dar al-Sharq.
1998. *Barnamaj al-Ittijah al-Muakiss* [The Opposite
Direction Program]. Doha: Dar al-Sharq.

Al-Afandy, Abd al-Wahab. 15 October 2002. "Tassfiya Qanat
al-Jazeera li-ta'oud al-miya al-arabiya ila mujariha."
[The refinement of Al-Jazeera: for hundreds of Arabs to
get used to its path." London: Al-Quds al-Arabi.

Al-Zaidi, Moufid. 2003. *Qanat al-Jazeera: Kassru al-Hurramat fy al-Faddai al-I'alamy al-Araby.* [The Al-Jazeera Channel: Breaking the forbidden in the Arab Media Space] Beirut: Dar al-Taly'a.

Allied Media Corporation. Official website. Alexandria, VA: <www.allied-media.com>

Alterman, John B. Spring 2005. "The Challenge for Al Jazeera International.' Cairo: *Transnational Broadcasting Studies* [TBS] *Journal.* 14: <www.tbsjournal.com/alterman.html> Spring 1999. "Transnational Media and social change in the Arab world" Cairo: *Transnational Broadcasting Studies Journal.* 2: <www.tbsjournal.com/Archives/Spring99/Articles/Alterman/alterman.html>

Amin, Hussein and James Napoli. 2000. "Media and power in Egypt" in Curran, James and Myung-Jin Park (eds.) 2000. *De-Westernizing Media Studies.* London: Routledge. 178-188.

Anderson, Jon. August 1995. "New Creoles of the Information Superhighway," *Anthropology Today* 11.4: 13-15.

Appadurai, Arjun. 1990. "Disjuncture and difference in the global cultural economy" in Featherstone, Michael (ed.) *Global Culture: Nationalism, Globalization and Modernity.* London: Sage. 295-310.

Associated Press (AP.) 24 March 2003. "Arab satellite station says stock exchange retaliates for war reports." Doha, Qatar: Associated Press.

Baatout, Faisal. 20 November 2004. "Al-Jazeera TV shakes up board as emir calls for professionalism" Doha: Agence France Presse.

Bahry, Louay Y. June 2001. "The New Arab Phenomenon: Qatar's Al-Jazeera" Washington: *Middle East Policy,* 8.2: 88-100.

Ballout, Jihad. 13-14 February 2005. Doha: Personal interview by the author of Al-Jazeera's spokesman.

Baudrillard, Jean. 29 March 1991. *La guerre du Golfe n'a pas eu lieu.* Paris: Galilée.

Borchgrave, Arnaud de. 7 May 2004. "Tutwiler's Mission Impossible." *The Washington Times.* Washington, DC: <www.washtimes.com/commentary/20040506-085117-7996r.htm>

Boyd-Barrett, Oliver. 2000. "Pan-Arab satellite television: the dialectics of identity" in Tumber, Howard (ed.) *Media Power, Professionals and Policies.* London and New York: Routledge.

Bradley, John R. April 2004. "Will Al-Jazeera bend?" London: *Prospect.* 97: 46-51.

British Broadcasting Corporation (BBC). February 7, 2000. "Interior minister comments on Arab media, relations with Yemen" BBC Summary of World Broadcasts. Part 4, the Middle East, Middle East Peace Process.

Burkholder, Richard. 12 November 2002. "Arabs favor Al-Jazeera over state-run channels for world news." Washington: Gallup Poll News Service.

Byrne, Ciar. 27 March 2003. "Al-Jazeera wins anti-censorship award." London: The Guardian. <http://media.guardian.co.uk/broadcast/story/0,7493,92 2496,00.html>

Campbell, Alistair. 15 September 2004. "I was wrong about al-Jazeera" London: The Guardian. < http://media.guardian.co.uk/iraqandthemedia/story/0,12 823,1304738,00.html>

Carey, James W. Summer 1993. "The Mass Media and Democracy: Between the Modern and the Postmodern" Columbia University: *The Journal of International Affairs.* 47.1: 1-21.

Carter, Bill and Felicity Barringer. 11 October 2001. "Networks Agree to U.S. Request to Edit Future bin Laden Tapes" New York: *The New York Times.* Sect. A, Column 4: 1.

Comor, Edward A. 1997. "The re-tooling of American hegemony: U.S. foreign communication policy from free flow to free trade" in Sreberny-Mohammadi, Ali et al. (Ed.) *Media in Global Context, A Reader.* London: Arnold. 194-206.

Curran, James and Myung-Jin Park. 2000. "Beyond globalization theory" in Curran, James and Myung-Jin Park (eds.) *De-Westernizing Media Studies.* London and New York: Routledge. 3-18.

Curran, James. 2002. *Media and Power.* London: Routledge.

Deacon, David, Pickering, Michael, Golding, Peter and Graham Murdock. 1999. *Researching Communications: A Practical Guide to Methods in Media and Cultural Analysis.* Oxford and New York: Oxford University Press.

Economist, The. 24 February 2005. "Arab satellite television: The world through their eyes." Cairo, Laayoune, Qatar and Ryadh: The Economist. <www.economist.com/world/displaystory.cfm?story_id =3690442>

El-Menshawy, Mustafa. 19-25 May 2005. "Live broadcast spurs Jazeera arrests." Cairo: *Al-Ahram Weekly* 743: Egypt 5. <http://weekly.ahram.org.eg/2005/743/eg5.htm>

El-Menshawy, Mustafa and Serene Assir. 24-30 March 2005. "Sick and suspicious." Cairo: *Al-Ahram Weekly* 735: International 1. <http://weekly.ahram.org.eg/2005/735/in1.htm>

El-Nawawy, Mohammed. Fall 2003. "Why Al-Jazeera is the Most Popular Television Station in the Arab World" New York: *Television Quarterly.* 34.1: 10-16.

El-Nawawy, Mohammed and Adel Iskandar Farag. 2002. *Al-Jazeera: How the Free Arab News Network Scooped the World and Changed the Middle-East.* Scranton, Pennsylvania: Westview Press.

Entman, Robert M. 1993. "Framing: Toward clarification of a fractured paradigm." *Journal of Communication.* 43.4: 51-58.

Olivia Qusaibaty

1989. *Democracy Without Citizens: Media and the Decay of American Politics.* New York: Oxford University Press.

Fandy, Mamoun. 4 July 2004. "Where's the Arab Media's Sense of Outrage?" Washington: *The Washington Post.* Final Ed., Outlook: B04.

30 March 2003. "Perceptions Where Al-Jazeera & Co. Are Coming From" Washington: *The Washington Post.* Final Ed., Outlook: B01.

Fukuyama, Francis. 1992. *The End of History and the Last Man.* New York: Free Press.

Gaballah, Ayman. 16 February 2005. Personal interview by the author with Al-Jazeera Deputy Chief Editor.

Gambill, Gary C. 1 June 2000. "Qatar's Al-Jazeera TV: The Power of Free Speech." *Middle East Intelligence Bulletin,* 2:5. <www.meib.org/articles/0006_me2.htm>

Ghadbian, Najib. June 2001. "Contesting the State Media Monopoly: Syria on Al-Jazira Television." *Middle East Review of International Affairs.* 5.2. <www.biu.ac.il/SOC/besa/meria/journal/2001/issue2/jv5n2a7.html>

Ghareeb, Edmund. 15 January 2001. "Thawra al-mo'alomat wa wasa'il al-itssal fy al-alim al-araby" [The power of information and mass communications in the Arab world] Dubai: *Al-Bayan.*

Giddens, Anthony. 1991. *The Consequences of Modernity.* Stanford: Stanford University Press.

Guaaybess, Tourya. Fall-Winter 2002. "A New Order of Information in the Arab Broadcasting system" Cairo: *Transnational Broadcasting Studies.* 9: <www.tbsjournal.com/guaaybess.html>

Hafez, Kai. 2001. "Mass Media in the Middle East: Patterns of Political and Societal Change" in Kai, Hafez (ed.) *Mass Media, Politics and Society in the Middle East.* New Jersey: Hampton Press.

Hallin, Daniel C. 1986. *The Uncensored War: The Media and Vietnam.* New York and Oxford: Oxford University Press.

Harding, Luke. 6 September 2004. "Iraq extends Al-Jazeera ban and raids offices." London: The Guardian. <www.guardian.co.uk/Iraq/Story/0,2763,1298039,00.html>

Harvey, David. 1989. *The Condition of Postmodernity: An Enquiry into the Origins of Cultural Change.* Oxford and New Malden, Massachusetts: Blackwell Publishers.

Hiebert, R. Eldon and Sheila J. Gibbons. 2000. *Exploring Mass Media for a Changing World.* London: Lawrence Earlbaum Associates Publishers.

Hirst, David. August 2000 b. "Qatar calling: Jazeera, the Arab TV Channel that Dares to Shock" Paris: *Le Monde diplomatique*, English edition. Pg. 3: <http://mondediplo.com/2000/08/08hirst>
9 April 2000 a. "The Television Studio Arab Leaders Hate the Most" Chicago, IL: *Chicago Tribune.*

Hiwar Maftouh [Open Dialogue]. 26 March 2005. "Hiwar Juma'at al-Muqawama al-Islamiya ma'a Washington." [Dialogue of the Islamic Forces Group with Washington.] Hosted by Ghassan bin Jeddo. Beirut: Al-Jazeera Satellite Channel. <www.aljazeera.net/NR/exeres/AE0FC9FD-Aab5-44B9-99F6-8A94F5FE6D49>
19 March 2005. "Al-Tahrak ash-Sha'aby al-'Araby." [The Arab Popular Movement.] Hosted by Ghassan bin Jeddo. Beirut: Al-Jazeera Satellite Channel. <www.aljazeera.net/NR/exeres/A887AE65-06DC-4C2C-AEAC-06BAA5330C64>
12 March 2005. "Intikhabat Ra'issiya Murtaqaba fy Iran." [The Anticipated Presidential Elections in Iran.] Hosted by Ghassan bin Jeddo. Beirut: Al-Jazeera Satellite Channel. <www.aljazeera.net/NR/exeres/C3A84A5F-59B5-40C7-92F9-6008B029B2ED>

5 March 2005. "Lubnan ba'ad Istiqala al-Hakuma wa Khotab al-Assad." [Lebanon after the Government's Resignation and [Bashar] Al-Assad's Speech.] Hosted by Ghassan bin Jeddo. Beirut: Al-Jazeera Satellite Channel. <www.aljazeera.net/NR/exeres/1ADE5827-CAAA-4338-9123-B799686BD7D6>

22 January 2005. "Mawqif 'Iraqi al-Kharij min al-Intikhabat." [The Iraqi Position after the Elections.] Hosted by Ghassan bin Jeddo. Beirut: Al-Jazeera Satellite Channel. <www.aljazeera.net/NR/exeres/76E388DE-B06D-45CA-9CF4-4A3C2A9E5629>

15 January 2005. "al-Tawtar al-Siassy fy Lubnan." [Political Tension in Lebanon.] Hosted by Ghassan bin Jeddo. Beirut: Al-Jazeera Satellite Channel. <www.aljazeera.net/NR/exeres/49CCAA09-A284-477E-AF8C-9CE85210E740>

8 January 2005. "Al-Mashad al-Intikhabat al-Filastany." [The Palestinian Electoral Scene.] Hosted by Ghassan bin Jeddo. Beirut: Al-Jazeera Satellite Channel. <www.aljazeera.net/channel/archive/archive?ArchiveId =111812>

1 January 2005. "Al-Mustaqbal al-Araby wa Qadiya al-Islah." [The Arab Future and the Issue of Reform.] Hosted by Ghassan bin Jeddo. Beirut: Al-Jazeera Satellite Channel. <www.aljazeera.net/channel/archive/archive?ArchiveId =111088>

Hoffman, David. March/April 2002. "Beyond Public Diplomacy" New York: *Foreign Affairs*. 81.2: 83-95.

Hoge, James. Summer 1994. "Media Pervasiveness" *Foreign Affairs*. 73.4: 136-44.

Huntington, Samuel P. Summer 1993. "The Clash of Civilizations" *Foreign Affairs*. New York: Council on Foreign Relations. 72.3: 22-28.

1996. *The Clash of Civilizations and the Remaking of the World Order*. New York: Simon & Schuster.

International Federation of Journalists (IFJ). 25 June 2004. "IFJ Condemns Ignorance and Inhumanity of White House as US Official Apologises to Media" Brussels: IFJ.

Jakobsen, Peter V. 2000. "Focus on the CNN effect misses the point: The real media impact on conflict management is invisible and indirect." *Journal of Peace Research*. 37: 131-143.

Keane, John. August 1991. "Democracy and the Media." *International Social Science Journal*. 43.3. 523-540.

Keohane, Robert O. and Joseph S. Nye. 2000 [3rd ed.] *Power and Interdependence*. New York, NY: Longman.

Kennan, George F. 30 September 1993. "Somalia, Through a Glass Darkly" New York: *New York Times*, A23.

Khader, Samir. 15 February 2005. Doha: Interview with Al-Jazeera Senior Producer.

Krane, Jim. 4 July 2005. "Al-Jazeera eyes West as it prepares to launch English-language channel." Doha: Associated Press. International News.

Kuttab, Daoud. 6 April 2003. "The Arab TV wars." New York: *New York Times Magazine*: 44-47.

Lamloum, Olfa. 2004. *Al-Jazira, miroir rebelle et ambigu du monde arabe*. Paris: La Découverte.
2003 (ed.) *Irak: Les médias en guerre*. Paris: Actes Sud.

Lil-Nissa' Faqat [For Women Only]. 28 March 2005. "Mashaqil al-muslimat al-gharbiat." [The difficulties of Western Muslim women]. Hosted by Louna ash-Shebl. Doha: Al-Jazeera satellite channel. <www.aljazeera.net/NR/exeres/DCDE4B73-8B32-448B-BF66-8DDD120B064B.htm>
14 March 2005. "Haq al-marat al-Kuwaitiya fyl-taswyt wal-turshyh." [The Kuwaiti woman's voting and candidacy rights]. Hosted by Louna ash-Shebl. Doha: Al-Jazeera satellite channel.

Olivia Qusaibaty

<www.aljazeera.net/NR/exeres/A27C5C0B-5AC3-
47B4-B86B-FE80B01B31B8.htm>
7 March 2005. "Mouatamr New York wa Haqouk al-
Mara." The New York conference and women's rights].
Hosted by Louna ash-Shebl. Doha: Al-Jazeera satellite
channel. <www.aljazeera.net/NR/exeres/419EF84F-
00C6-40C2-869D-5A4ECD7E4DDD.htm>
31 January 2005. "Al-tarbiya al-janssiya lil-Atfal."
[Sexual education for children]. Hosted by Louna ash-
Shebl. Doha: Al-Jazeera satellite channel.
<www.aljazeera.net/NR/exeres/4CE817E8-39B9-
4AE7-AF88-2D3C719E20E5.htm>
24 January 2005. "Thaqafa al-3amal al-tattwa3y lidaa
al-jam3iyat al-khairiya al-nissaiya" [The culture of
voluntary work in women's charitable organizations].
Hosted by Louna ash-Shebl. Doha: Al-Jazeera satellite
channel. <www.aljazeera.net/NR/exeres/A800E58B-
EA5E-4D17-98FE-124CFEDB1F85.htm>
17 January 2005. "Al-istighlal al-janssy lil-atfal." [The
sexual exploitation of children]. Hosted by Louna ash-
Shebl. Doha: Al-Jazeera satellite channel.
<www.aljazeera.net/NR/exeres/D4A20A61-882C-
4033-89B2-2D13A3881C99.htm>
11 January 2005. "Istikshaf Isarar al-banat."
[Discovering girls' secrets]. Hosted by Fairuz Zayani.
Doha: Al-Jazeera satellite channel.
<www.aljazeera.net/NR/exeres/C25B2698-4C04-
4D89-AE5D-2372DF7BF8AE.htm>
3 January 2005. "Al-A'aradd al-mutarabissa bil-najin
min kariya Tsunami." [Future diseases for the Tsunami
survivors]. Hosted by Fairuz Zayani. Doha: Al-Jazeera
satellite channel.
<www.aljazeera.net/NR/exeres/221AC639-BE32-
4D8D-A477-ED36B36D3BBA.htm>
Livingston, Steven and Todd Eachus. October-December 1995.
"Humanitarian Crisis and U.S. Foreign Policy: Somalia

and the CNN Effect Reconsidered" *Political Communication*. 17: 413-429.

Lokmane, Samia. 11 May 2005. "Iqra', Al Jazira, ces "chaînes" cathodiques arabes," Tunis: *Liberte*. <www.liberte-algerie.com/edit.php?id=38873>

Lycos 50. 1 April 2003. "This Week's Lycos 50." Pittsburgh, Pennsylvania: <http://50.lycos.com/040103.asp>

Mathews, Jessica. 8 March 1994. "Policy vs. TV" *The Washington Post*, A19.

McCombs, Maxwell E. and Donald L. Shaw. Summer 1972. "The agenda-setting function of the mass media." *Public Opinion Quarterly* 36: 176-187.

McLuhan, Marshall. 1964. *Understanding Media: The Extensions of Man*. London: Routledge & Kegan Paul.

Miladi, Noureddine. 2003. "Mapping the Al-Jazeera Phenomenon" in Thussu, Daya Kishan and Des Freedman (eds.) *War and the Media: Reporting Conflict 24/7*. London, Thousand Oaks, and New Delhi: Sage Publications. 149-160.

Miles, Hugh. 2005. *Al-Jazeera: How Arab TV News Challenged the World*. London: Abacus.
1 September 2004. "The Spirit of Saddam." London: The Guardian. Analysis section. <www.guardian.co.uk/Iraq/Story/0,2763,1294713,00.html>
17 April 2003. "Watching the War on Al-Jazeera: Watch Both Ways." London: London Review of Books. 25.8.

Mill, John Stuart. 1869. *On Liberty*. London: Longman, Roberts & Green.

Mohammadi, Ali. 1998. "Electronic empires: an Islamic perspective." In Thussu, Daya K. (ed.) *Electronic Empires: Global media and local resistance*. London, New York, Sydney, Auckland: Arnold. 257-273.

Mroue, Bassem. 4 September 2004. "Iraqi government decides to extend closure of Al-Jazeera's office in Baghdad." Baghdad: Associated Press.

Noujaim, Jehane (dir.) 2004. *Control Room.* New York:
    Magnolia Pictures, 83 minutes. English and Arabic with
    subtitles. With Sameer Khader, Lt. Josh Rushing, Tom
    Mintier, Hassan Ibrahim, David Shuster and Deema
    Khatib.
Newspaper Association of America (NAA) 21 July 2004. *Facts*
    About Newspapers 2004 Vienna, VA: Newspaper
    Association of America.
New York Times, The. 30 March 2003. "Why Al Jazeera
    Matters." New York: Editorial. Late Edition – Final,
    Sec. 4, P. 12. Col. 1.
O'Neill, Patrick H. 1998. *Communicating Democracy: The*
    Media and Political Transitions. Boulder, CO: Lynne
    Rienner.
Pan Arab Research Center. Visited January-February 2005.
    Dubai: <www.arabiandemographics.com>
Power, Carla and Reem Haddad. 8 August 2005. "Look Who's
    talking" *Newsweek* Atlantic Edition. 50-54.
Psenny, Daniel. 20 May 2005. "Al-Jazira annonce le lancement
    d'une chaîne en langue anglaise en 2006," Paris: *Le*
    Monde.
Miller, John. May 1998. "Interview: Osama bin Laden." New
    York: ABC News. Obtained from the Public
    Broadcasting Service (PBS) website on 16 April 2005:
    <www.pbs.org/wgbh/pages/frontline/shows/binladen/w
    ho/interview.html>
Reporters Without Borders/ Reporters Sans Frontières. Cited
    12 August 2005. "War in Iraq." Paris: Reporters sans
    frontières. <www.rsf.org/special_iraq_en.php3>
Reuters. 14 March 2005. "Spain Frees Ill Al Jazeera Newsman
    to House Arrest." Madrid:
    <www.reuters.com/newsArticle.jhtml?type=topNews&
    storyID=7895518>
Robinson, Piers. 2002. *The CNN Effect: The myth of news,*
    foreign policy and intervention. London and New York:
    Routledge.

Rush, Robin D. 31 January 2005. "Readers Pick Apple: 2004 Readers' Choice Awards" New York: *Brandchannel.* <www.brandchannel.com/features_effect.asp?pf_id=248>

Saad, Lydia. 23 April 2002. "Al-Jazeera viewers perceive West differently." Washington: Gallup Poll News Service. <www.gallup.com/poll/content/default.aspx?ci=5860>

Said, Edward W. 1979. *Orientalism.* New York: Vintage Books.

Sahmoud, Sami. 21 January 2005. London: Personal interview by the author with former aljazeera.net journalist.

Sakr, Naomi. Fall 2002. "Seen and starting to be heard: women and the Arab media in a decade of change." *Social Research* 69.3: 821-850.
2001. *Satellite Realms: Transnational Television, Globalization and the Middle East.* London and New York: I.B. Tauris Publishers.

Saleh, Heba. 24 December 2004. "US pressure 'delayed UN Arab report.'" London: *Financial Times.* 4.

Sheikh, Ahmed. 20 February 2005. Doha: Personal interview by the author with Al-Jazeera Editor-in-chief.

Schiller, Herbert I. 1969. *Mass Communication and American Empire.* New York: A.M. Kelly.
1976. *Communication and Cultural Domination.* White Plains, NY: International Arts and Sciences Press.
1996. *Information Inequality: The Deepening Social Crisis in America.* London: Routledge.

Schleifer, Abdallah S. Fall 2004. "Al Jazeera Update: More Datelines from Doha and a Code of Ethics." Cairo: *Transnational Broadcasting Studies Journal.* 13: <www.tbsjournal.com/aljazeera_schleifer.html>
Fall 2000. "A Dialogue with Mohammed Jasim Al-Ali, Managing Director, Al-Jazeera." Cairo: *Transnational Broadcasting Studies*: <www.tbsjournal.com/Archives/Fall00/al-Ali2.htm>

Shannon, Claude E. and Warren Weaver. 1963. *The Mathematical Theory of Communication.* Urbana and Chicago: University of Illinois Press.

Siebert, Fredrick S., Theodore Peterson and Wilbur Schramm. 1956. *Four Theories of the Press: The Authoritarian, Libertarian, Social Responsibility, and Soviet Communist Concepts of What the Press Should Be and Do.* Urbana: University of Illinois Press.

Smith, Graeme. 29 March 2003. "Pentagon downed Web site, Al-Jazeera editor says." London: Saturday Globe and Mail. <www.globetechnology.com/sevlet/story/RTGAM.200 30329.uhack0329/GTStory>

Souag, Mostefa. 26 November 2004. London: Personal interview of Al-Jazeera's London Bureau Chief and Senior Correspondent by the author.

Telhami, Shibley. 2005. *Reflections of Hearts and Minds: Media, Opinion, and Identity in the Arab World.* Washington: Brookings Institution Press. 29 April 2004. "Hearing on the Broadcasting Board of Governors: Finding the Right Media for the Message in the Middle East." Washington: United States Senate Committee on Foreign Relations. <http://foreign.senate.gov/testimony/2004/TelhamiTesti mony040429.pdf>

Thussu, Daya K. 1998. "Localising the global: Zee TV in India." In Thussu, Daya K. (ed.) *Electronic Empires: Global media and local resistance.* London, New York, Sydney, Auckland: Arnold. 273-295.

Tomlinson, John. 1997. "Internationalism, globalization and cultural imperialism" in Kenneth Thompson (ed.) *Media and Cultural Regulation.* London: Sage.

United Nations Development Program (UNDP). 5 April 2005. "Arab Human Development Report 2004: Towards Freedom in the Arab World." <www.rbas.undp.org/ahdr2.cfm?menu=12>

UNESCO Institute for Statistics (UIS). July 2004. *Literacy rates, youth (25-24) and adult (15+), by country and gender for 2000-2004*. Paris: <www.uis.unesco.org>

U.S. Embassy to Indonesia, Public Affairs Section. October 18, 2001. "Defense Secretary Rumsfeld Interviewed by Al-Jazeera." U.S. Embassy Press Release. Jakarta: <www.usembassyjakarta.org/press_rel/Rumsfeld.html>

U.S. Department of State. 23 February 2001. "Country Reports on Human Rights Practices – 2000: Qatar." Washington: U.S. Department of State. 2000: 815. <www.state.gov/g/drl/rls/hrrpt/2000/nea/815.htm>

USInfo, Middle East and North Africa. 9 August 2004. "Defense Department Report, August 6: Rumsfeld on Al-Jazeera" Washington: U.S. Department of State. 2004: 490718. <usinfo.state.gov/mena/Archive/2004/Aug/09-490718.html>

11 February 2003. "Iraq, al-Qaida 'Bound by a Common Hatred,' Says Boucher." Washington: U.S. Department of State. 2003: 137. <usinfo.state.gov/xarchives/display.html?p=washfile-english&y=2003&m=February&x=20030211185341sk aufman@pd.state.gov0.5013697&t=xarchives/xarchite m.html>

Varoudakis, Aristomene and Carlo Maria Rossotto. February 2004. "Regulatory reform and performance in telecommunications: unrealized potential in the MENA countries." *Telecommunications Policy*. 28.1: 59-79.

Wallis, William. 16 May 2005. "Al-Jazeera to launch English language TV channel in 2006," Cairo: *Financial Times*. USA Ed. 1: World News 6.

Warf, Barney & Grimes, John. April 1997. "Counterhegemonic Discourses and the Internet." *Geographical Review*, New York: American Geographical Society. 87.2 : 259-274.